BURN BABY, BURN!

D0474171

RECORDING AUDIO CDs
FROM ANY SOURCE, LPs TO MP3s

Peachpit Press
Berkeley, California

Burn, Baby, Burn! Recording Audio CDs from Any Source, Vinyl LPs to MP3s

Peachpit Press
1249 Eighth Street
Berkeley, CA 94710
510/524-2178   800/283-9444   510/524-2221 (fax)

Find us on the World Wide Web at: www.peachpit.com
To report errors, please send a note to errata@peachpit.com
Peachpit Press is a division of Pearson Education

Editors: Jennifer Eberhardt and Karen Reichstein
Project Editor: Michael Thurston
Technical Editor: Stephen Nathans
Copyeditor: Darren Meiss
Compositor: Gloria Schurick
Indexer: Lisa Stumpf
Cover Design: Mimi Heft
Interior Design: Kim Scott (kim@bumpy.com)

ISBN 0-321-24131-2

9 8 7 6 5 4 3 2 1

Printed and bound in the United States of America

Contents at a Glance

To whomever I'm dating right now.
—Josh

To Mom and Dad.
—Bob

Acknowledgments

The authors wish to thank Kenny and Angie Abeyta, proprietors of Sebastian's Grill (located at the intersection of Broadway and Bayaud, in Denver, CO). We'd also like to express gratitude to Julio Romero, Jeff O'Connor, and Diablo for keepin' those rounds and breakfast burritos coming on the rough days. A special thanks goes out to Johannes, proprietor of Sooper B Liquors (also located on the corner of Broadway and Bayaud, in Denver, CO), whose unwavering trust that we'd pay him back another day saved us from nervous breakdowns. Props to all the hardware and software manufacturers that sent us stuff; without that, of course, there'd be no book. Many thanks to the production staff who put this book together (Hi Maureen! And Jeff! What happened?), and endless thanks to Steve Nathans, Karen Reichstein, and Jennifer Eberhardt for tidying up the long string of foul adjectives and nouns that constitute Josh's typical speech. Last but not least, thanks for the records, Suzi Post.

About the Authors

Josh McDaniel is a columnist and regular contributor for *EMedia* magazine, though it has been remarked that what he submits could hardly be termed "regular." When trying to trace the length and exact content of his freelance career, Josh finds he cannot—due to a dissolute youth, he can't remember much of anything antedating yesterday. He remembers writing for *Wired* a little while back, and a handful of other magazines. He also remembers being the co-author of *The Little Audio CD Book*.

Bob Starrett has been a contributing editor and columnist for *EMedia* magazine since 1995 and covers the CD-recordable and digital audio technology markets. This will be his sixth co-authored book on the subject. Bob is considered one of the world's leading experts on CD recording technology and has acted as an expert witness in many CD- and DVD-related court cases.

Table of Contents

Introduction

Bob said, "I know! Let's call it 'Burn, Baby, Burn!'!" Josh said, "No! No book with my name on it shall invoke disco, especially that song." (It's called "Disco Inferno" by the way.) Josh got edified, thanks to Bob.

Turns out the phrase "Burn, Baby, Burn!" was what a young, talented, razzle-dazzle, black DJ named The Magnificent Montague used to say before he'd spin a record at the station. He'd yell it out over the airwaves, and the kids who loved his soul-music show would call in and yell it back at him. This dates back to 1963, when Bob first started collecting Social Security.

Then, in August 1965, when The Magnificent Montague was working at KGFJ in Los Angeles, he awoke one morning to see an uprising in the streets of Watts on the TV news and to find his record-spinning rallying cry at the center of it all. Activists, radicals and other sensible people had taken "Burn, Baby, Burn!" for their own, using it in reference to the conflagration in L.A. It became a revolutionary slogan.

Upon hearing that, Josh immediately acquiesced to the title "Burn, Baby, Burn!" for this book.

The story continues that The Magnificent Montague had a crisis of conscience. He had a huge stake in the Civil Rights Movement, but wondered, for some stated reasons and other reasons we're left to speculate upon, whether or not he should continue using "Burn, Baby, Burn!" as his introduction to the track lists set before him.

The reasons for this crisis of conscience seem obvious. There's violence during revolutionary times, and many, if not most people find violence abhorrent and would never wish it committed in their name (Rodney King, for instance). And a guy's gotta eat: it's easy to see why a job might hang in the balance if The Magnificent Montague continued spinning after that utterance.

We wonder, though, if there was another reason that The Magnificent Montague had a silent thought. Using the phrase in conjunction with radio might minimize the struggle for justice the lower and marginalized classes were engaged in, "Burn, Baby, Burn!" might have grown larger than The Magnificent Montague, and you, and me.

Pondering that, we decided to announce here that the last thing we wish to do is minimize the ongoing struggle for real justice in this country, and in the world. On the contrary, we wish to announce our allegiance to Angela Davis, Kwame Toure, George Jackson, Huey Newton, and anyone else who might have shouted "Burn, Baby, Burn!" in a revolutionary spirit.

We're of the opinion that humanity is something worth preserving, especially now, in this time of unilateral wars conducted by illegitimate presidents, and unthinkable, egregious exploitation of the whole world—First through Third—by transnational corporations under the auspices of the least democratic entity ever to roam the earth, the WTO.

Though we face the same constraints The Magnificent Montague did, we did our best to write this book in a revolutionary spirit, and somehow managed to get "Burn, Baby, Burn!" on the cover. (Bob did the dissembling, and Josh played dumb.) If it stays there, and if you preserve some obscure record album or MP3 doomed to be excluded from the next digital canon (as CD did to many important artists and people), we've done all we set out to. Josh still won't be happy, though.

—Josh McDaniel

—Bob Starrett

Diving Right In

I n the grand tradition of Western Epic, after Homer, Virgil and Milton, we shall begin in the middle of things—*in medias res*, as the Latins would put it. We expect to find you rarin' to burn, but not sure of the next step, your will in search of a way. With that in mind, we'll begin with a whirlwind tour of the recording process.

We'll also start by assuming a few more specific things about you:

○ You don't have a chitinous shell protecting your innards (see Figure 1.1).

○ You've got music stored on some kind of medium, whether that be an old, battered record or a hard disk.

○ You've got a computer, with a drive capable of recording CDs.

and

○ You'd like to use that drive to create audio CDs.

Beyond that, we assume nothing, and won't cast any judgment about genres, bands, songs, operas, or concertos. We'll talk more about the how, why, what, and where than The Who.

1.1 We're landlocked and, consequently, cannot get a live photo of a Rock Lobster, so this photo of Goldie The Rock Lobster Cat will have to do.

Our book concerns itself primarily with acquiring music from any of several sources, converting it to a digital format as needed, then moving that music (or speech, or whatever sonic stuff you like) over to CD-R in a manner that conforms to the CD-Audio standard. You may then play these creations in your car stereo, your home entertainment system, or your boom box in the park over slow-roasted chicken filets, coleslaw, beans, and a nice Chardonnay. (We recommend Kendall-Jackson, a bountiful mid-range bottle, more toward butter than oak, at least in the recent vintages.)

NOTE

We're going to go ahead and use "recorder" or "burner" in place of "CD-R/RW, DVD-R/RW, DVD+RW, or other device capable of recording CDs." It's not laziness; it's just that we don't want to go through every writable drive out there when we have to refer to your recording device. That would get on everyone's nerves, we're guessing (and Josh is easily confused to boot).

That said, here we go.

Find Your Tunes

As we mentioned, we assume you've got some music lying around. In this book, we'll show you not only how to get this music to CD (by *burning* it, as it's commonly known), but also how to transform your analog material—vinyl records and cassette tapes—into digital audio. We'll also show you how to edit, clean, and sweeten digital audio, as well as a few funky things you can do with your creations.

NOTE

The difference between analog and digital material boils down to this: analog material—such as the songs on a record or cassette tape—is recorded and played back in time, chronologically. Digital material, the music on your CDs, for example, is a binary representation of analog material that is interpreted by your playback device back into analog material.

There are many big advantages to CD-Audio, but two in particular stand out here: binary data isn't fettered by time (which is why you're able to select a track to play with the touch of a button), and nothing except the light of your playback device's laser touches the CD, which results in little wear and tear, if any. "But my CD skips!" you say. That's the fault of the manufacturer, or possibly even you, naughty person. By the way, in Chapter 3, "Copying Audio CDs," we'll show you how to fix a skipping track.

Some of you kept the vinyl. Good on you. No matter what, it's worth something, either in a sentimental, financial, or just plain "it sounds good" sense. One of the wonders of vinyl-to-CD transfers is that you can actually make it sound *better*. Two chapters address the intricacies of this process. The first is **Chapter 2, "Hardware and Software,"** where you'll find a couple things you need for that kind of project, specifically a preamp and digital audio editing software. (You may have those things already and you just don't know it, or you may have to go get those items, in which case we've got a bunch of recommendations.) And in **Chapter 7, "Recording and Restoring Vinyl,"** we'll show you how to preserve these treasures by copying them to CD and, if you have the inclination, how to digitally remaster them, removing clicks, pops, hiss, and even scratches.

Dollars to doughnuts, we'll bet you own at least one music CD. In **Chapter 3, "Copying Audio CDs,"** we'll show you how to duplicate any CD in your collection, as well as how to extract (also known as *rip)* single tracks so that you may move them into a compilation CD. It's been our unfortunate experience that one good song on the radio doesn't translate into a good 11-track CD. In fact, that one good song is often the only good song on said CD, which is reason enough to start improving your CD collection by consolidating the keepers.

TIP

If you're leaving CDs lying around outside of their jewel cases, sleeves, and so on, leave them music-side (the shiny side) down. Contrary to popular belief, air and exposure to the elements will do more damage to your CD than a tabletop or carpet.

If you've downloaded (legally or not) any music from the Internet, you're probably already familiar with the term *MP3*. Ah, MP3, that small item that's pitted the record industry against, well, pretty much everyone else alive on Earth, including bands, fans, and 12-year-old honor students. We'll touch on the furor briefly—along with industry-sanctioned MP3 sources—in **Chapter 4, "Recording MP3s to CD,"** but we'll focus primarily on how to "decode" MP3s so they can be written to CD.

Got a favorite Internet radio station? You can easily record streaming audio and burn it to CD for later listening. **Chapter 5, "Capturing and Recording Digital Streams,"** shows you what you need to know.

Time was when cassette tapes outsold records and CDs, and you probably bought your share in those strange transitional times. Tapes are really easy to work with. In **Chapter 6, "Restoring and Recording Cassette Tapes,"** you'll learn how to transfer your tapes to CD, with only a minimal amount of digital restoration necessary.

Prep 'Em

The audio CD is a fascinating little creature, to us, anyway. Keep in mind we're kinda weird, according to relatives, friends, and loved ones. Bob, for example, on seeing Figure 1.1, shook his big booty but good, and started singing the words "Rock Lobster" in a castrato falsetto that caused Josh's ears to bleed.

In terms of how CD-Audio data is written and read, it's nothing like a CD-ROM, or a DVD, or anything else for that matter. There's a very specific format for CD digital audio, described in a technical document called the Red Book. Ironically, this particular Red Book was not written by Chinese communists; it was written by Sony and Philips. It's an incredibly boring read, so, if you're going to read a Red Book, we suggest you read the one by Mao Tse-Tung instead.

We'll begin with the easy stuff. We'll show you how to rip tunes that already accord with the CD-Audio standard, that is, tracks that are already on CDs. (See Chapter 3 for that.)

Next, we'll move over to the Internet, where music exists in abundance but must be altered in some fashion or another before it's ready for CD-R. (It's not at all complicated, so have no fear.) For example, if you wish to capture your favorite Internet radio station's Reggae Hour, we'll show you how to record it to your hard disk, transform it into "data" suitable for CD-Audio, split it into tracks, and burn it to CD-R. (See Chapter 5 for that.) MP3s, too, receive no small treatment in Chapter 4; there, we'll show you how to "decode" an MP3 so that it may be burned to CD.

After that, we'll show you how to "digitize" cassette tapes and records, so that they may be restored, preserved, and enjoyed. Things get slightly more complicated there, but, again, it's not quantum physics. (Or, actually, it is, but you don't need to know anything about quantum physics to restore your records and tapes.) The only new issue that arises is you'll be working with analog material, and, consequently, you'll need to make a couple hardware connections so that the analog material can be digitized, edited, sweetened, and split.

Interesting Stuff You Don't Need to Know

The Red Book sets forth two standards for CD digital audio: one for structure and one for content, known as "physical" and "logical," respectively.

The logical standard of the Red Book sez:

○ Your "data" (music) must be nabbed via PCM. PCM (Pulse Code Modulation) is a means devised to represent analog material—such as a live jam session—digitally, that is, transformed into the 1s and 0s of binary.

○ Your data must be sampled at 44.1 kHz. That means 44,100 "listenings" of the band's live jam are taken every second. We'll go into more detail about these "listenings" in Chapters 6 and 7, where we actually digitize analog material.

○ Each sample must consist of 16 bits, which is binary information about what the "listening" heard during sampling. This is where the analog material becomes digital material.

This binary information gets "demodulated," or translated, back into analog in what's called a "pulse code demodulator," which, in this book anyway, is a fancy way of saying CD player.

A PCM 44.1 kHz, 16-bit item goes by *.wav on a PC and *.aiff on a Mac, with the asterisk standing in for whatever the tune is called. What we're going to be doing in this book is either extracting or decoding WAVs and AIFFs from digital sources, or actually making WAVs or AIFFs from analog material, specifically, your records and tapes.

The Red Book, named for the color of its binder, was followed by several other CD books (not necessarily in chronological order here): the Yellow Book (CD-ROM specs), the Orange Book (CD-R specs), the Blue Book (Enhanced CD specs), the White Book (VCD specs), and the Green Book (CD-i specs, if anyone remembers that miserable failure of an idea). In this book, we'll be treating of the Red, Orange, and Blue books.

Burn 'Em

There's a "How" in addition to the "What" described earlier: audio CD tracks must be written to CD-R in a very specific fashion. Fortunately, your CD recording software knows how; matter of fact, it knows how to write any disc according to any CD standard. If you want a CD-ROM, it knows how to do that; if you want a Video CD, it knows how to do that. It knows, so you don't really have to.

There are a couple options you have when burning audio CDs—one of which we'll discuss here, because it's among the most important options you'll be offered—but these are simple choices, and we'll talk about them in detail when they arise. For now, we'll show you a simple, standard burn by using a couple standard tracks we've got on this hard disk.

More Interesting Stuff You Don't Need to Know

The physical standard laid out in the Red Book is simple: Lead In, Tunes, Lead Out.

The Lead In contains the audio CD's Table of Contents (that's the technical name for it, believe it or not), the information about what tune—or "track," more properly—is where on the disc. It's very much like the Table of Contents of this book: it points you to the collection of words you wish to read. The Lead Out of an audio CD, for all intents and purposes, is a chunk of nothing that indicates to the laser that the disc is over.

Now things are going to veer a bit: this book concerns itself not with listening to CDs, but rather restoring, sweetening, compiling, and above all, recording CDs, so that you can listen to them later. We're entering the realm of the Orange Book, the CD-R standard. This is where the work comes in.

Fear not: the software you use (or will procure after having a look at your choices in Chapter 2) to record CDs knows all about how to write things according to their physical standards. What you'll need to do is tell your software how and what to record. In all but Chapter 9, "Creating Enhanced CDs," this is a simple matter of telling your software you intend to make an audio CD and where your tracks are, and then clicking some button or other. If that doesn't work, we'll point you toward Chapter 10, "Tips, Tricks, and Troubleshooting."

For this example, we're going to use Roxio's Toast 6 Titanium (www.roxio.com) on a Mac, as shown in Figure 1.2. (Again, have a look at Chapter 2 for your Mac and PC CD-R software options.) If you have a Mac, you probably have some version of Toast or other software. (Roxio likes to ship limited versions of its software in the hopes that you'll buy the mega-package.) If you're working with a PC, stay with us here: the procedure we're about to run through is pretty much the same in all CD recording software, whether it's on a PC or Mac. These days, all you have to do to burn an audio CD is inform your software you intend to burn an audio CD, drag some tracks somewhere that says "Drag Tracks Here," click a burn button, and you're mostly done, save for a couple options you'll be given in a burn dialog.

1.2 Using Roxio's Toast 6 Titanium. You can see we've selected the audio CD tab up top and selected the audio CD radio button off to the left.

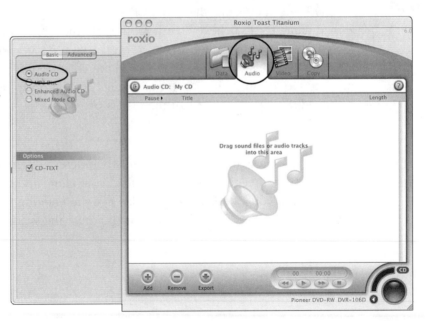

1. You'll want to start by opening Toast, like we did, or by opening whatever software it is that you prefer using.

2. To get your tracks queued up for the burn—in this instance, a handful of tracks from Easy Star All-Stars' *Dub Side of the Moon*—click the Add button and navigate on over to your tunes (see Figure 1.3). From the list of tracks, drag and drop whatever you like into the "Drag sound files or audio tracks into this area."

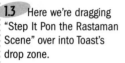 **1.3** Here we're dragging "Step It Pon the Rastaman Scene" over into Toast's drop zone.

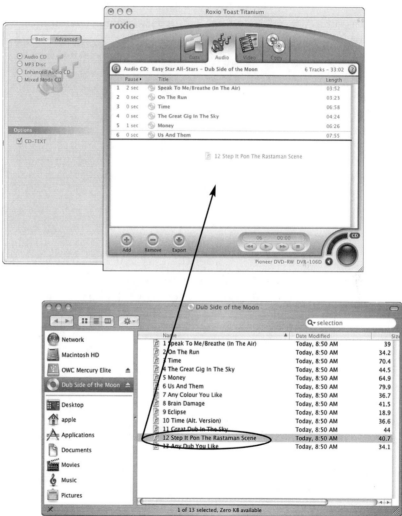

3. When you're satisfied with what'll be on your disc come burn time, punch the record button—the big round thing (see Figure 1.4).

1.4 Most software has a pronounced button someplace that you'll click when you're ready to burn. Toast is a prime example: see that big ol' thing in the lower-right corner?

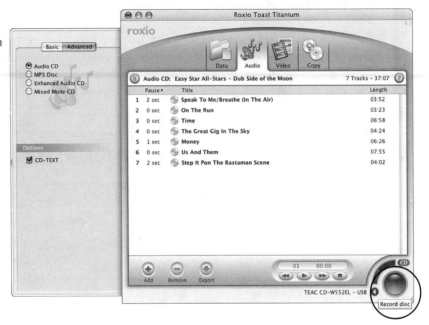

4. This summons a simple burn dialog box (see Figure 1.5), where you'll select your recorder (here a TEAC), a recording speed (we selected Best, but Best isn't always best as you'll see in the ensuing chapters), and how many copies of this particular CD you'll want (just one here).

1.5 In all but a few instances, clicking the big burn button brings up a dialog asking you anywhere from 3 to 30 final questions. We'll tell you the answers as they come up.

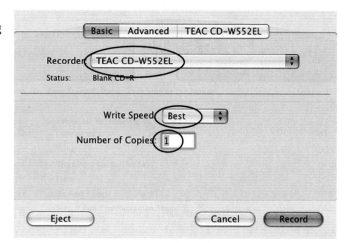

One final thing we'll need to address directly here before we click that Record button is the difference between Track-at-Once and Disc-at-Once recording. (We'll talk about this in a little more detail in Chapter 2.) Typically, when you indicate you're ready to write, your software will hurl up a set of options for you. You may be asked for

○ A write speed (12x? 40x? 52x? What? See Chapter 2 for "X" stuff.)

○ Whether or not you wish to test the burn procedure before you commit anything to disc

○ Whether you wish to enable a buffer underrun protection scheme (Again, see Chapter 2 for info on these.)

○ How many copies you want

    or

○ All of the above.

Then, in most cases (all cases, if your recording drive was purchased within the last three years or so), there'll be an option to write DAO (Disc-at-Once) or TAO (Track-at-Once). In Toast, you'll find these options under the Advanced tab in the burn dialog. (Toast defaults to DAO.)

TAO versus DAO

TAO is good for one thing: you don't have to finalize your disc. This way, you can leave the disc laying around for years, amassing tunes and burning them until the disc is full. By nature of the writing scheme, two seconds of silence will be introduced between whatever tracks you have lined up during the burn. This is great for neatly trimmed tracks with no silence at either end—you can go ahead and finalize a disc with those types of tracks, if you want to. The disadvantage, and this is a big one, is that discs that aren't finalized can't be played in your standard CD player, whether that's a home entertainment system component or a changer in a car. It can, however, be played in the CD recorder you use to burn the disc.

DAO is the way to go in almost all cases. You can have your software put just about any amount of silence between your tracks, and if it's the case you've created a crossfade or want a butt splice (see Chapter 8, "Polishing Your Compilation CD"), you can have your software leave absolutely no silence between those particular tracks. You could even have four seconds of silence between two tracks, two seconds of silence between another two tracks, and then no silence between another two tracks all on the same disc. It's up to you, and we'll show you how.

5. Now all you have to do is put a piece of blank media in your recorder and click the Record button in the lower-right corner of the burn dialog (see Figure 1.5).

Shortly, you should have a bona fide audio CD that you can play anywhere—car, picnic boom box, home entertainment center, wherever (see Figure 1.6).

NOTE If you met with failure, have a look at Chapter 10 (it's directed primarily at PC people, since they work with an OS that to this day still devotes every single resource possible to writing even a floppy). Few things go wrong on a Mac here, but if they do, Chapter 10 will serve Mac users as well, but in a more general sense.

1.6 Success! This doesn't happen all the time, so don't get those hopes too high. We'll do our best to see to it that you are successful more often than not, but even we, the "experts," blow a disc now and again.

That's all there is to it. Pretty Simple, eh?

A Word of Caution, or Make That Two Words

First word: naturally, you'll be listening to loud stuff. Please be very careful with your ears, seriously. Feedback—that horrible (except in the case of Jimi Hendrix) high-pitched noise when an input device receives its own signal from an output device—is a possibility in some of the procedures we'll be showing you. Feedback can cause permanent damage to your hearing, which is why you'll find Josh beating up sound booth guys who don't know what they're doing. We'll warn you, of course, when it comes up, but do try to keep your ears' health in mind at all times.

Second word: you'll be working with copyrighted material. Infringement on copyright is against the law—anyone who's ever rented a movie has seen the FBI warning regarding that particular issue. Neither of us condones the use of drugs, but one drug offers a convenient analogy: to be on the safe side, treat your creations like joints. (Those are marijuana cigarettes, by the way, for those unfamiliar with the term.) You're probably not going to get busted for having a joint, especially if you relegate this activity to your home, and even if you do get caught with a joint, it's not going to be a huge deal, other than the slightly uncomfortable brush with the law. If you get busted selling many, many joints, or carrying pounds of marijuana around in public in a big lawn and leaf bag, you're in more than a little trouble. Outside of that, we leave all else to your conscience.

A Note from the Publisher

Whether you do it one time or a million times, infringement of copyright is against the law. Period. Peachpit Press does not condone copyright infringement under any circumstances.

A Note from Josh and Bob in Response to the Note from the Publisher

While we are at variance on other copyright issues, we are together on this one: it's our contention that sometimes copyright *must* be infringed upon in order to preserve our culture, history, and heritage. Hundreds of thousands, if not millions of old recordings never made it into the CD canon, and never will. They'll vanish into oblivion if someone doesn't digitize, restore, and preserve them. In our time, precisely the same thing will happen: millions of artists worth preserving will be left behind by whatever post-CD medium the record companies decide upon.

Will you decide what gets preserved, or will you let corporate America decide for you? We're guessing the former, and that is precisely why we wrote this book.

As Michael J. Anderson says in *Twin Peaks,* "Let's rock."

Hardware and Software

Here's where we get to turn the Military Industrial Complex against itself. In this chapter we're going to talk about things the military secretly developed to kill people, so that you can publicly turn out insubordinate CDs to stop them from killing people (or at least CDs that can be pumped up way too loud for the comfort of the Death Lobby's hairy ears). You got laser-guided bombs? We got laser-guided Dead Kennedys (which we count as cool, except for the fact Jello continues to be hosed by his former bandmates).

Didja know: The very first laser was created in Jello Biafra's hometown, at the University of Colorado, Boulder? That Josh went to CU Boulder, but he didn't know that the very first laser consisted of a synthetic ruby and a flash tube until way after he left? That Josh is eighty-sixed from every bar in Boulder, except the Sundown Saloon?

It's a good bet you already have most—if not all—the things you need to turn out an excellent CD. If you don't, fear not: the things we imagine you don't have are either free or inexpensive. One thing we'll have you do is try what you have first; then, if you're unhappy, upgrade.

Your Arsenal

Let's quickly run through what you should have:

○ One drive capable of recording CDs. Optionally, you may want another optical drive for disc-to-disc copying.

○ Media (blank CDs).

○ CD recording software. This probably came with either your drive or as part of the software on your prefab machine.

○ A Digital Audio Editor (DAE), which you may already have as part of your CD-R software package, but might not know it.

○ A sound card or USB audio capture device. We can say with pretty good certainty you have the former.

○ A tape deck and a turntable—but only if you wish to embark on tape or vinyl restoration and recording projects.

○ RCA cable, detailed in Chapter 7, "Restoring and Recording Vinyl," and/or Y cable, discussed in both Chapter 6, "Restoring and Recording Cassette Tapes," and Chapter 7.

○ A preamplification device. This is necessary only for vinyl restoration and recording, and might be something you already have, but might not know it.

○ A computer speaker system. You've probably got those already.

○ Headphones. These are optional—unless you have a spouse, you live under a covenant in a condo, or your neighbors are mean—in which case they're a necessity.

NOTE

If your neighbors call the police with a noise complaint, and the police come to your door, you can waylay them very easily. First, they do not have probable cause to enter your home (unless, when you open the door, they see a firearm or incendiary device) and cannot cross the threshold, or order you to turn your music down. At this point all you need do is talk with them outside your home, or simply tell them to go away until they secure and can produce a warrant.

Second, they'll need to measure the "noise," and bring that measurement to a judge, who may or may not issue a search warrant. Only with a warrant will the police be entitled to enter your home.

By the time all that happens—if it happens at all—you should be done with whatever you're working on and your home should be relatively quiet, leaving the police frustrated by an informed citizen. They hate informed citizens—ask Josh.

Just in case you lack any of the abovementioned items, or are confused by any of those terms, we'll detail each in this chapter. This is designed as a reference chapter more than anything: skip around as you please. For example, if you already have a CD recorder you're happy with, go ahead and skip the "Recording Drives" section. There are tidbits in each section that'll enlighten, possibly entertain, but it's not necessary to read this chapter all the way through.

Recording Drives (CD-R/RW, DVD-R/RW, DVD+R/RW, and so on)

What if you don't own a burner and need to buy one? What if you have a burner, but it dates from the late '90s (see Figure 2.1), and its rate of recording brings to mind phrases like "waiting for paint to dry," "molasses in January," and "dogged progress of a tapeworm through my large intestine?" We're lousy with intestinal fortitude here, though we'll probably leave the gastroenterology to the experts. But have no fear, if it's burning woes you're having—the CD kind, that is—we'll talk you down and get you through it. Here are a few distinctions and tips that may help you when you go shopping for your first burner, or perhaps a replacement for a broken or older and slower one.

2.1 This is what CD recorders used to look like, circa 1989.

TIP

Your biggest concern at this point should probably be paying too much. If you drop more than $99 on a new CD recorder—we're talking high-speed, top-of-the-line—or more than $199 on one that also writes DVDs, you are, well, getting burned.

Five years ago, this would have been a long, drawn-out discussion of various considerations. Luckily, today, recording technology has evolved to the point where there is little to consider, and almost any available recorder will work well for your audio recording projects (see Figure 2.2).

All of today's CD and DVD recorders write to two kinds of CD media: CD-Recordable (CD-R) and CD-Rewritable (CD-RW). Of course, DVD burners write several kinds of DVD media, too—as well as CD-R and CD-RW—but other than huge MP3 discs, we have little concern for DVD in the audio arena.

2.2 This, of course, is what recorders look like today.

The obvious advantage of CD-RW is that you can write to it multiple times, whereas you can only write to CD-R once. But for our purposes, the benefits end there. For one thing, you can usually pick up CD-R media for about twenty cents a disc or less in bulk (even "free" with the ever-present rebates), and a CD-RW disc usually costs a little more. What's more, you can write a CD-R disc significantly faster than a CD-RW disc.

Most importantly, since our goal is to make discs that we can play on our stereos, CD-R is the obvious choice. Although some CD-Audio players and most current DVD players will play CD-RW discs, this is not true of many CD-Audio players and earlier DVD players and also of many car CD players. (As for car DVD players, we're going to pretend you didn't ask.)

NOTE

On the other hand, if you bought one of the first 60,000 or so DVD players sold in Japan in 1997 or the U.S. in early 1998, you might have bought one that played CD-RW and *not* CD-R. If so, you have a collector's item on your hands, which means you should probably put it in a trophy case somewhere, donate it to a museum, or just cash it in and buy a new one that will read more formats for less money.

The good news is, all current CD-ROM and DVD-ROM drives—which probably describes what you have in your computer—will play back both CD-RW and CD-R discs.

So, although we realize that many companies now use the term "CD Recorder/Rewriter"—or worse, persist in describing their offerings only as CD-RW drives—we'll stick with the horses that got us here. Again, any drive you buy that has the Compact Disc ReWritable, DVD+ReWritable, or DVD-R/RW logo on the faceplate, or some combination of the three, or was sold to you as anything ending in "RW," will write CD-R, which is all we really care about here. From this day forward, we will refer to the drives, whether CD or DVD, that can write audio CDs only as recorders, or, when we feel like letting it all hang out, as burners. In the audio recording context, at least, the world will be better for it.

The Need for Speed

Going all the way back to the early days of CD recording, CD burners have had unseemly names, like the DW-S114X and AID+840G. This has only gotten worse as the drives have mastered more read and write formats, which has added more clumsy verbiage to their names. Today, in addition to those unwieldy model numbers, you'll see recorders advertised in what seems at first to be a confusing string of Xs. And you'll see terms such as 16x10x40, and 40x12x48, and 52x32x52, and—worst of all—8x8x4x2x40x24x48. What does this all mean? (For the moment, let's disregard the last one—those first four numbers are a bunch of DVD stuff that's not our concern.)

It looks complicated, but it ain't. Let's tackle 40x12x48, and break that one down. There are three things, CD-wise, that a recorder does:

❍ The first is write CD-R media. (That's the 40.)

❍ The second is write CD-RW media. (That's the 12.)

❍ The third is read CD-R and CD-RW media and pressed CD-ROM discs. (That's the 48.)

So, to break it down simply, the first number is the maximum speed at which the recorder will record CD-R media. The second number is the maximum speed at which the recorder will write CD-RW media. The third number is the maximum speed at which the recorder will read CD-R, CD-RW, and CD-ROM media, except for audio discs, of course. Audio discs are never played at more than 1x, unless you want G.G Allin to sound like Alvin and the Chipmunks.

The "Max" Factor

Why do we say "maximum speed?" It's like this: the first several generations of CD recorders actually wrote data to disc at the same speed across the span of the disc. These were called *constant linear velocity*, or *CLV*, recorders. This was great news for users and product marketing people alike because, for once, it meant that the marketers were actually relating accurate information. A 12x CLV drive wrote at 12x, period. But CLV maxed out at 12x, which meant if recorder manufacturers wanted to get past it, they had to take a different approach.

Today's CD recorders use one of three writing methods: constant angular velocity (CAV), zoned-constant linear velocity (Z-CLV), and partial constant angular velocity (P-CAV). CAV is the easiest to understand. Imagine a skater doing a triple axle, or if you don't know exactly what that means (we don't either), just spinning around with her arm extended. In terms of distance covered over time, which is half of velocity (the other is direction, which we're not gonna worry about right now), her outstretched fingers are traveling faster than her elbow, which is traveling faster than her shoulder, which is traveling faster than her head, and so forth. This, essentially, is constant angular velocity.

For recorders to achieve constant linear velocity, they actually had to spin faster when the laser was writing at the inner hub of the disc (where CD recording begins), than at the outer edge (where recording ends), to do so at equal speeds. (Same thing with reading the data back.) CAV recorders spin at the same speed throughout, and by doing so, write faster at the outer edge because the write laser is covering more territory once it's working in that area.

This means a couple of things: one, a recorder whose maximum write speed is 52x is probably writing around 24-32x at the inner hub, and doesn't achieve full 52x until it's writing the last portion of the dataset, which means, say, minutes 72-80 of an audio disc, if you're actually filling it up. For a full disc, the "52x" recorder might average about 40x, which is pretty doggone fast—if 1x is 80 minutes, that's two minutes total. The difference between that and 80 divided by 52 (the time elapsed for "true" 52x; we'll leave the higher math to you), probably isn't something you'll notice.

continues

continued

Z-CLV works somewhat differently. As the name suggests, the recorder divides the disc into zones, and records at a constant speed throughout each zone. P-CAV writes at incrementally increasing speeds for awhile, like CAV, then levels off. In each case, as with CAV, the recording starts at one speed, finishes at another, operates at several other speeds in between, and averages out somewhere in the middle. We'll leave it to your friends in the marketing department to draw out those distinctions further. We're sure they'll be happy to oblige.

Guts in the Machine

Internally, a CD-Recordable drive (or a DVD drive that records CDs) is similar to a standard CD-ROM or DVD-ROM drive. Because all recorders today not only write but also read discs, much of the mechanics are similar.

A recorder physically consists of an optical head, a turntable for the disc, a controller, and a signal-processing system. The optical head, which shines the laser on the disc surface, is mounted on a sled or swing arm and includes a laser diode, a lens, and a photodetector that reads the laser reflections from the disc (see Figure 2.3). The laser is capable of different power settings: a low setting (.5 milliwatt) used when reading a disc, and a high setting (4 to 8 milliwatt) used when writing to CD-R media. The photodetector contains several photodiodes that ensure the laser beam is in focus and following the disc track, or pregroove.

2.3 Overcoming fear of recorders is a simple matter of popping one open. It's a pretty simple device, mechanically speaking: a laser rides a sled to grandmother's house, shooting off light amplified by stimulated emission of radiation (Einstein's idea) to alter the dye of a recordable disc spinning overhead.

A *pregroove* is a microscopic spiral track on the disc that guides the laser as it writes data. Drive electronics direct the laser beam to focus on a portion of the disc. As the laser pulses according to the data being fed to the recorder, the heat generated by the laser causes the organic dye on the CD-Recordable disc to deform, creating optical marks that are interpreted by a CD-ROM or CD-Audio player as the pits that would be formed had the disc been injection-molded. These marks are read by a CD-ROM drive or audio player in the same manner as pits on mass-replicated discs, even though they are created by a different process. A multifunction controller in the drive handles the focus, tracking, turntable motor rate of spin, and input from user controls.

The Interface

If you're buying a computer nowadays, you will likely end up with an internal IDE recorder (see the following sidebar for more on IDE). Whether it is DVD or CD, it uses the same interface as your hard drive; in fact, it may plug into the same cable, depending on how many IDE devices you have in your computer. Or if you are using a Mac, options will vary by model—SCSI for early Power Macs and the first Power Mac G3-based systems; USB for early iMacs; USB and FireWire for more recent iMacs; and USB, FireWire, IDE, and SCSI for Power Mac G4s and G5s. (It's worth noting, though, that the recent G4 and G5 towers won't let you add a standard half-height IDE drive to the second bay—round hole, square peg—so you're basically stuck with the drive that came with it unless you want to add one externally.) PC users can use USB and FireWire, too, although IDE still accounts for the majority of recorders on the PC side.

The Big Secret About USB and FireWire Drives

Ever wonder why USB and FireWire recorders are external only? Well, the reason is simple. The recorders themselves are nothing more than standard IDE recorders, and the magic occurs in the external case in which is mounted a circuit board that interprets the USB and FireWire signals into those that an IDE drive can understand.

If you already have a recorder or extra recorders and want to make them USB or FireWire devices, you can purchase, for a reasonable price, an external case that will magically convert your drive to USB or FireWire without having to purchase another recorder.

One thing to keep in mind about USB: there are two versions, 1.1 and 2.0. Both are fast enough to record CD-Rs, but USB 1.1 will max out at 8x, so if you attach a 48x drive to a USB 1.1 port, it will connect, but it won't record at anywhere near full speed. USB 2.0, standard on many new machines and available as a $29 PCI add-on card just about anywhere computer items are sold, will let you kick out the jams with your speedy CD recorder.

Name That Connection

When we say IDE, we mean IDE, EIDE, ATA, and ATAPI because they are all generally the same thing, just an interface specification. The terms are bandied about haphazardly enough, generally by marketing types, that it's easier and just as useful to say IDE (Integrated Device Electronics) than to distinguish this from EIDE (Enhanced Integrated Device Electronics) and ATA (AT Attachment) and ATAPI (AT Attachment Packet Interface). Anything we say here in reference to IDE will apply no matter which of these acronyms you happen to encounter when you're researching various CD or DVD recorders.

In whatever incarnation, and whatever it is called, IDE is just a simplified way of connecting hard drives, CD-ROM drives, CD recorders, DVD-ROM drives, DVD recorders, and other peripherals to a computer. Let's do it this way: on a PC, look at the cable that connects to your hard drive. That's an IDE cable. Your motherboard usually has two IDE connectors. You can plug two IDE devices (hard drives, CD-ROM drives, CD recorders, DVD/CD recorders) into each cable. With one other step that we'll get to in a minute, that's all you need to know. Plug that cable into your recorder. Forget ATAPI, ATA, and EIDE. The only other thing you need to do, and do this first, is to set the Master/Slave jumper on the back of the recorder. The back of an IDE recorder has three jumpers: Master, Slave, and Cable Select, sometimes marked C/S. Forget Cable Select altogether. Never think of it again or inquire as to its use.

Because the IDE cable will take two devices, make sure that one is set to Master and the other is set to Slave. To be safe, set your recorder as Master on the second IDE cable, if you can.

Media (Blank CDs)

Although 74-minutes (650MB) used to be the standard capacity of CD-R discs, most media you'll see today will be labeled 80-minute, or 700MB. This is great for the audiophile because you can get more music on a disc. The latest "advance" in media capacity is to 99-minute discs, but we don't recommend them because of various potential compatibility problems. Still, you are free to experiment with them if you like. Just remember, even if you can record them, most recorders will only burn them out to 89:59; few will go to the full capacity. And even if your recorder and software are able to burn these discs, you must do it at a much reduced speed, thereby increasing recording time considerably.

Again, our advice is not to use these discs. Seventy-four and 80-minute media are fine; 99-minute media is asking for trouble.

The Orange Book specification (see Chapter 1, "Diving Right In") for recordable media defines the standards to which the discs must conform, but does not determine the process by which the blank discs are manufactured. Manufacturers may use different, often proprietary, processes to create the media. Manufacturers are constantly experimenting with the formulas for the organic dye polymers in the discs; and even with the same formula and even under stringently controlled conditions, there can be variation between production batches of dye polymer.

There are also variances in how well different brands of media perform in different brands of CD recorders. Although rare, it still happens. The same drive that produces flawless recorded discs with one type of media sometimes produces a "coaster"—that all-too-descriptive term for a failed CD-R disc—from another type of media. It is also possible to create a CD-R disc that works on one CD-ROM drive or audio player but not another.

There Are No Stupid Questions, Only Stupid Answers

Sometimes people ask—and this isn't a stupid question if you've never worked with CD recorders—whether a disc recorded at 52x, for instance, can be read by a drive that only reads at 24x or in an audio player that plays at only 1x.

The answer is yes: no matter what speed a disc is recorded at, it can be read at any other speed in the case of a CD-ROM. With an audio disc, it will play in any audio player at 1x, no matter what speed was used to record it.

Dyes

CD-R makers use several different formulations of organic dye when creating the recording layer of CD-R media—the most popular being phthalocyanine and metal azo. You can recognize phthalocyanine-based media by its bright emerald green color (that is, when it is on media with a gold reflective layer—the dye itself is blue). Phthalocyanine-based media is yellow-green in color (again, on a gold-backed disc—otherwise, it's just pale green). Metal azo dye is identified by its deep blue color (this time if it's on a silver-backed disc—it is green otherwise). A variation, the aqua-hued advanced phthalocyanine, is also now in wide use. You can easily identify CD-RW media by its gray color. Manufacturers use two types of reflective layers—gold and silver—on recordable discs. Yes that's real gold and real silver there on the disc, but don't be fooled. Although not as painful as scooping out your fillings to sell the precious metals therein, trying to scam gold or silver from CD-Rs is just as pointless. However much gold or silver a CD-R may contain, it's not enough to make them cost—or be worth—much more than a buck each, if that.

Using CD-RW Media for Audio Discs

We thought you'd never ask…. Can you use CD-RW media to make audio discs? Sure you can. You can make them all day long and play them all day long in your CD-ROM drive. But when it comes to playing them in your car stereo or on your home stereo, you are probably in for a surprise. They won't work. Why not? Because the reflectivity of a CD-RW disc is much lower that that of a CD-R disc, and CD-Audio players, except for some very recent ones, do not have the correct lasers to read the disc properly. Sometimes you can get lucky and a well-made player will actually pick up on the disc despite the reflectivity difference, but we don't think that we are really that lucky, neither having yet won the lottery.

CD-RW can be useful for setting up an audio disc without making a lot of CD-R discs that you don't quite like, however. With CD-RW, you can make your disc, listen to it on your computer, erase it if you are not happy, and then do it again until you get it just right. Then you can just copy the CD-RW disc to CD-R and have a nice, finished product. But if you follow the other advice in this book and carefully extract, clean, and listen to your audio files before committing them to disc, you can usually get it right on CD-R the first time around.

You notice that we said you have to erase the disc and do it over. Why can't you just erase a single track and replace it? The answer is that you can, but only if it is the last track on the disc. Once you erase the last one, the next to the last one becomes the last one and you can erase that, too, all the way down to the first track. Why can't you erase something in the middle? Because whatever you put in its place is unlikely to be the same length as what you took out, and there is no provision for shifting things around like you can with a MiniDisc, for instance.

CD-R Software

You have lots of choices for software for recording audio CDs, from the cheap hack to the professional package, from the subterranean, download-only marvel to the mass-market monolith. What's important to you in a CD recording package? The number one consideration, in our opinion, is that the program has the versatility and power you need to make great music discs and works well on your machine.

The capability of the user's machine to keep up with the demands of the recording process has always been a problem. To get around these system limitations, many programs use proprietary drivers to try to keep the process stable but end up causing recording conflicts and problems. For one thing, the drivers themselves are often unstable. What's more, some programs have trouble coexisting with one another. So if you have three recording packages installed on your machine, you might have some problems.

Roxio's ubiquitous Easy CD & DVD Creator 6 (www.roxio.com), for example, can get pretty territorial once you invite it onto your machine. For the safest recording experience, stick to one program each for ripping, editing, and recording. You may find a program that performs all three functions well, and if that is the case, and it works for you, stick with it. We are not discouraging you from experimenting with many programs, however, nor are we suggesting that you must necessarily limit the programs that you keep handy on your hard disk. Just keep in mind that the possibility of conflict is high, probably more with CD recording tools than with any other type of software.

To circumvent any of these potential hang-ups, figure out exactly what you need to rip, edit, and record, and make your decision from there.

NOTE

Chances are that you got some recording software when you bought your recorder. Or if you bought a machine with a recorder pre-installed, some pre-installed software came along for the ride. Most recorders come with software for recording data and music, although many times it is a "lite" edition and does not have all the features that you might want. (Easy CD Creator is a good example of that—although the bundled version basically does the job, you have to upgrade to the "Deluxe" edition to get all the audio recording features.) If not, check out the next section.

Recording Software for Windows

The good news here is that most of the other software you may need to acquire to round out your audio toolset is free or inexpensive (a notable example being Nero Burning ROM 6.0). Of course, if your tush gets tense in coach and you must fly first-class, by all means flash your platinum card around town and buy yourself some high-end tools. Gold-plate your keyboard while you're at it. But few of us need to make a major investment in software to get good-quality audio discs.

NOTE — Apple's iTunes is yet another piece of software you can grab, but since it was originally created for the Mac, we've covered it in the "Recording Software for Mac OS" section instead of here."

Easy CD & DVD Creator 6
Roxio, $99 (www.roxio.com)

Roxio Easy CD & DVD Creator 6 is easily the most widely installed CD recording tool in the market today—no surprise, since it comes pre-installed with loads of CD recorders and recorder-equipped PCs. It's got a solid arsenal of audio tools, although you need to upgrade to the full version to have access to them all. **Audio Central**, for ripping CD tracks, assembling and sequencing CD compilations, and applying gain normalization and recording them to disc, is straightforward and easy to use. **Disc Copier** is a handy utility for bit-for-bit disc copies.

Sound Editor, formerly known as CD Spin Doctor, handles analog recording tasks. It offers some interesting audio clean-up and manipulation tools like declicking and "room simulator," and will detect silences between tracks and allow you to cut and paste sound clips, but it should not be mistaken for a full-fledged professional audio editor. Roxio was the first company to include a Spin Doctor-like utility in a mainstream recording tool, so they deserve some credit for that.

Roxio was also the first recording tool vendor to combine CD and DVD recording, as well as basic CD authoring in a consumer tool, which has brought DVD authoring software guys like Sonic and Ulead into the CD recording space, theoretically giving users more options.

2.4 Roxio's Sound Editor, née Spin Doctor, trying out a cool enhancement called Room Simulator.

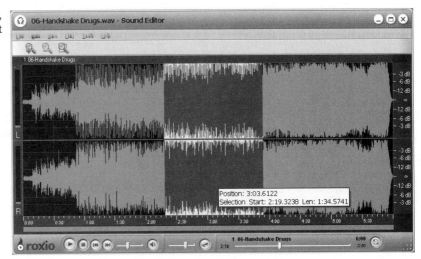

Nero Burning ROM
Ahead Software, $69 (www.nero.com)

Ahead's Nero has been Josh's favorite from the get-go, and not just because it's named after the dude who may or may not have fiddled while Rome burned. (A sucker for a good-ol' fiddling hoedown, and no fan of empires, Josh is willing to give him the benefit of the doubt.)

Now in **Nero 6 Ultra Edition**, Nero is a jam-packed product suite, with the all-purpose **Burning ROM**, a lite version called **Express** (there's another one that may have come with your recorder), **NeroVision Express** for DVD authoring, a disc-labeler, two handy drive-testing utilities (keep those close at hand), and two audio-specific tools, SoundTrax and Wave Editor. You'll do your music-disc copying, compiling, and burning in Burning ROM, and you can also make enhanced CDs here, as described in Chapter 9.

We're especially big fans of **SoundTrax**, the analog audio recording tool, which enables you to easily create crossfades (just drag one track over the next), cut and loop your tracks, and apply effects from Nero **Wave Editor**, the audio editing tool. The easy give-and-take between SoundTrax and Wave Editor makes us wonder why we all can't get along.

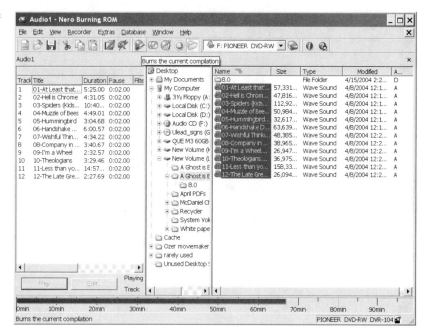

2.5 Assembling a music compilation in Nero. Drag and drop. Cool Record button. Nuthin' to it.

CD & DVD Maker 6.7
NewTech Infosystems, $49 (www.ntius.com)

NTI's CD & DVD Maker doesn't get quite as much play as Creator and Nero, but it's got some interesting audio features. Its **Live Audio** module lets you burn straight to CD from analog sources, basically anything coming in from your sound card, line-in, or microphone. Bob engineered one of the first-ever direct-to-disc live recordings during the CD Jam at SIGCAT '98 in Baltimore; it would have been a lot easier with Live Audio.

You can also do all the standard CD-Audio compilation and disc copying stuff in CD-Maker: TAO, DAO, the works. CD-Maker also has **Wave Editor**, with a nice Amplify feature that's much more helpful with especially quiet tracks than the Normalize feature you find in most of these tools.

2.6 Let's boost up Amy Righy's "Are We Ever Gonna Have Sex Again?" so we can hear the words. "I looked for your id today, seemed that id had gone away." Much better.

RecordNow! Deluxe
Sonic Solutions, $49 (www.sonic.com)

RecordNow! Deluxe (formerly a Veritas product, and Prassi Europe before that) was bought by Sonic Solutions and quickly integrated into its **MyDVD** authoring package. Unfortunately, Sonic's **RecordNow! Deluxe** is the limited version formerly known as RecordNow DX, which is a mere shell of the former RecordNow Max, a truly fine CD recording tool worthy of its inventors, Umberto Bassignani and Paolo Barettani, who basically invented CD recording software.

The Sonic version wears MP3-like skins and is reasonably audio-centric, but makes it virtually impossible to tell where your extracted tracks go if you don't burn 'em right to CD. Very restrictive, very limited.

If you can get your hands on Stomp RecordNow Max 4.5, consider snapping it up and doing your audio recording there. If not, go with one of the other three tools we just described.

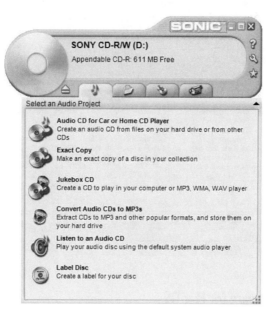

2.7 Sonic's RecordNow Deluxe, not what it used to be.

Burn.Now
Ulead Systems, $99 (www.ulead.com)

Burn.Now, the newest product on this list, ships as part of Ulead Systems' **DVD MovieFactory 3 Disc Creator** bundle, again part of the recent trend toward combining consumer DVD authoring and CD recording in a single tool. It's not as versatile and full-featured an audio recording tool as Creator, Nero, or CD-Maker, but it costs about the same as those tools. And if you bought MovieFactory for the DVD authoring, and your main goal, CD-wise that is, is to make some compilations from CD tracks, you probably don't need to venture outside Burn. Now.

If you select Create Music Disc from the opening wizard, you'll have three choices: audio CD, MP3 CD, and MP3 DVD. Pick one, and enter the main Burn.Now windows, where you select Add Files and go through the usual Explorer navigations to find your tracks. Pretty straightforward stuff, right down to the red Record button.

2.8 Burn.Now also lets you add CD-Text information if you're so inclined.

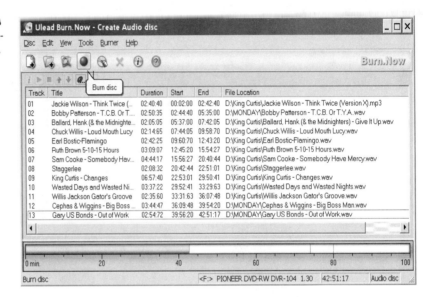

Recording Software for Mac OS

Things aren't quite so diversified on the Mac side, but then again they never are. Time was when nearly every company in the Windows market had a Mac version, but these were mostly afterthoughts, mere shells of their Windows counterparts. The good news: this didn't make much difference to Mac users. For one thing, Mac recording was always pretty straightforward and pre-dictable (much more so than Windows recording back in the day), and the dominant tool, Toast, was bundled with most Mac drives and did the job as well or better than the rest.

The popularity of CD recording has seen the development of other new soft-ware, so once again, Mac users have choices. Many may opt to stick with iTunes, the software that ships with just about every new Mac these days, which is just how Apple would want it, control freaks that they are.

iTunes 4
Apple Computer, free (www.apple.com)

Unlike the other Mac recording tools, iTunes sets out to be more than simply a piece of CD burning software. It's a jukebox, it's a digital music store, it syncs with Apple's iPod, and it's freely available for both Macs and Windows-based machines. But if we're going to (heh-heh) compare Apples to apples, best to stick to what it does in the CD burning arena.

iTunes defaults to the factory-installed SuperDrive, but it's compatible with most newer external CD and DVD drives. Don't even bother trying to install another internal drive; the new G5 makes it impossible, and the older G4s have drive bays set up so that most drive trays won't slide out of the front of the machine. The app makes it ridiculously easy to rip audio discs to AIFF or MP3, although you have to go into Preferences to make the switch, which is an unnecessary step.

Speaking of unnecessary steps, iTunes won't copy a disc from the SuperDrive to an external drive—you've got to rip the files to the hard drive first, then burn them with either the SuperDrive or the external drive, which just about cancels out any speed gains you might be hoping to get out of a 48x or 52x external. That's just dumb. And even though iTunes' Playlist function is a great organizational tool, you can't rip tunes directly into a new Playlist. So, if you want to make a copy of Tarbox Ramblers' *A Fix Back East*, you need to rip the tunes into the master library, then create a playlist, and *then* drag all your tunes to the new playlist. Then, and only then, can you burn those tracks.

The biggest difference between iTunes and the other Mac CD burning software is, of course, the iTunes Music Store, which you get access to whether you want it or not. It's a reasonably priced way to get your hands on music quickly, at $.99 a song. Apple puts limits on how many times you can burn a particular playlist, but there's no limit on how many times you can burn each AAC track to CD. (And here's iTunes' dirty little secret: Once you get the track on a disc, you can convert it to MP3 or AIFF or any other format you want.)

Oh yeah, there's also one other little difference: iTunes is free, and comes preinstalled on all Macs.

2.9 An iTunes compilation CD, ready to burn.

Toast 6 Titanium and Toast with Jam 5
Roxio, $89-$189 (www.roxio.com)

By and large, any Mac user who ventures beyond iTunes for Mac CD recording opts for **Toast Titanium**. And with good reason—it's a powerful, intuitive tool. It's better integrated than it used to be; the old Toast Extractor is built into the main interface now, and the product also features **CD Spin Doctor** (a named borrowed from old versions of Easy CD Creator), a fine tool for recording analog audio.

Toast with Jam adds, as you might guess, Jam, a more sophisticated recording tool for more intensive hobbyists. With Jam, you get configurable, hexagram-like crossfades representing the different ways tracks can overlap (looks like something from the *I Ching*—roll the coins before fading for best results); a gain lever for fine-tuning; and **BIAS Peak LE VST**, the best entry-level audio recording and editing tool in the Mac world.

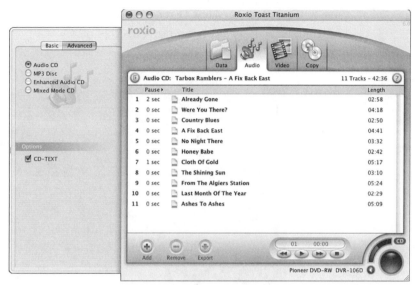

2.10 Here's Toast. Note the between-track silences on the left, which you can change with a click of the mouse.

Dragon Burn for OS X
Newtech Infosystems, $49 (www.ntius.com)

Dragon Burn is a good alternative to Toast if you're determined to buck the Roxio behemoth. It doesn't offer all the DVD recording stuff that Toast does at this point, but we don't really care about that here. It does DAO, TAO, enhanced CD, MP3 CDs from iTunes playlists, and so on, in a nice, facile manner. It also suggests a "Smart Burning" speed to keep you from overestimating your Mac's capability to support a fast burn.

On the other hand, you might wonder why they bother, since the maximum speed they offer is 16x—fine if you're recording to the internal SuperDrive, but a major disappointment if you've got a 40x burner on the FireWire bus. Buffer underrun protection seems to slow things down even more.

One of the banes of Mac CD recording—immutable and mysterious—is drive recognition. Dragon Burn circumvents this nicely with its Dynamic Drive Support, a big boon for Mac users.

Here's Dragon Burn with Smart Burning enabled. Check out the 16x max speed. Hang onto your hat!

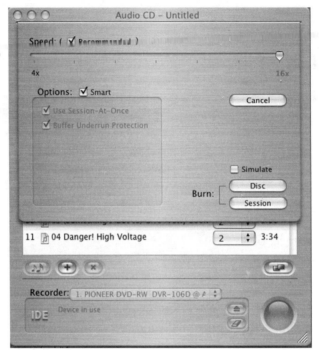

Digital Audio Editing and Restoration Software

Many CD recording packages today include at least a rudimentary digital audio editor, if not one capable of restoring old recordings. So, it's likely you already have a digital audio editor on your machine, either as part of your prefab computer's preloaded recording software, or part of the software bundle that came with the recorder you bought. Try these out, and if you're unhappy with your current digital audio editor—Roxio's offering is a little disappointing, for example—there are other, better stand-alone digital audio editors out there.

Nero Burning ROM's latest iteration comes to mind. For $69, it features not only the finest CD recording utility around (Josh's opinion—ed.), but also a fully functional digital audio editing/restoring utility—Nero Wave Editor. It also features a multitrack utility, Nero SoundTrax, which makes crossfading and multiple file normalization available to you. (See Chapter 8, "Polishing Your Compilation CD," for details.)

2.12 Nero's latest iteration comes complete with a digital audio editor and a multitrack utility. Can't beat it for the price.

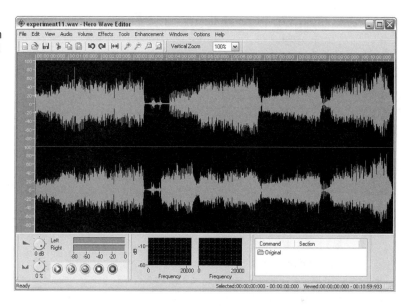

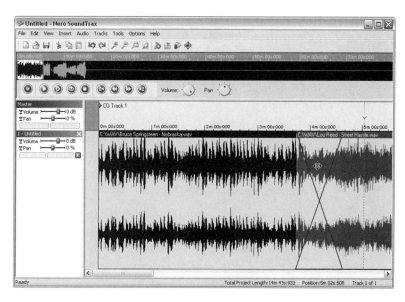

The following are digital audio editors both of us recommend. They've undergone rigorous testing at the lab here, and we can say with good certainty that they'll never do you wrong. Most of the companies that manufacture the digital audio editors listed offer free trial downloads, too, so you know precisely what you're getting.

For the PC

Diamond Cut Millennium, $59
Diamond Cut Productions, Inc.
www.diamondcut.com

DC 5, $199
Diamond Cut Productions, Inc.
www.diamondcut.com

Audition 1.0, $299
Adobe Systems, Inc.
www.adobe.com

SoundForge 7.0, $399
Sony Pictures Digital, Inc.
mediasoftware.sonypictures.com

For the Mac

HyperEngine-AV, $99
Arboretum Systems, Inc.
www.arboretum.com

Deck 3.5, $399
BIAS, Inc.
www.bias-inc.com

Logic Platinum 6.0, $699.95
Apple Computer, Inc.
www.apple.com

Digital Performer 4.1, $795
MOTU, Inc.
www.motu.com

Filters You'll Want to Master

These filters (some project-specific) are standard restoration filters. Play with—and thereby train yourself—until you're comfy with them. (We'll talk about how to configure each through the course of this book.) We don't have your ears, so we can't say what makes you happy—this is where your work comes in.

Gain Normalization, Normalization (and, in One Instance, Volume Leveling)   This filter brings all your tracks up to a standard "loudness" so that no one track leaps out at you as being too loud relative to the rest of your tracks. This is the simplest filter to work with, and will be used on all compilation CDs.

Reverb   A reverb filter helps to bring life back to a dead-sounding track. If you do decide to hit a track with reverb, make sure your dead-sounding track isn't dead-sounding because of overapplication of other filters. Reverb can be used on anything you like, be it a decoded MP3 or a less-than-bright record side.

Equalizer   Equalizers come in handy when you're unhappy with, say, a bass-bereft MP3, or you just want your track to sparkle a little more. These are the digital equivalents of what you may have attached to your home entertainment center. We'll use equalizers on compilation CDs in this book in Chapter 8, where we'll be working with tracks from various sources (MP3s, restored vinyl, restored cassettes, and so on).

DeHiss, DeNoise, Continuous Noise Filters   This filter is your bestest buddy when you're working with tapes and records. It removes—this sounds tekkie, but it ain't really—low amplitude noise across the frequency spectrum. In Chapters 6 and 7, we go into great detail about the Continuous Noise filter.

DeClick, Impulse Noise Filters   This filter is designed to remove the clicks and pops characteristic of vinyl recordings. By far, this is the most difficult filter to configure—you have to precisely describe to the filter the nature of the clicks and pops you're facing—so many times, people simply mute the clicks and pops. Clicks and pops happen so suddenly, and over such a short time, you can mute them with impunity—your ear, by design, won't miss anything.

Median Filter   If it happens your continuous noise filter didn't get rid of the crackle inherent to vinyl recording (it's that campfire noise), a median filter will do the trick. This is another difficult filter to configure.

High-Pass, Rumble Filters If it happens your stylus is "bottoming out" (making contact with the bottom of a record groove) or if your turntable introduces mechanical noise, run a High-Pass filter. Rumble (it sounds like, well, rumble) exists at a very low amplitude—so low that nothing else but rumble could exist there—it's easy to be rid of. We'll show you how in Chapter 7.

DeHum, DeBuzz, Notch Filters If you hook up your cassette or record player rig correctly, you probably won't have to deal with this filter at all. If you do—possibly because the equipment used to make the recording added hum to it—it's not at all hard to get rid of it. Hum exists at a very specific frequency, so all you'll have to do is name your frequency, and then run the filter.

Possibly Requisite Stuff, Depending on What You're Up To

With the exception of the section "Computer Sound Systems," you need the following items only when you're recording analog material to your hard disk, in preparation for burning to CD. Though it'll work just fine, the sound card you have isn't necessarily the best sound card for capturing analog audio, so we'll discuss some upgrade options here. As far as tape decks, turntables, and preamplifiers go, they're cheap and easy to find (if you don't already have them). Finally, computer sound systems are requisite for all projects (you need to be able to hear what you're doing, right?), but as we'll tell you, you don't need to upgrade to an expensive array. The two speakers you probably already have will do just fine.

Sound Cards and USB Audio Capture Devices

We're pretty sure you've got a sound card (see Figures 2.13 through 2.15): it's what you plugged your multimedia speakers into. Sometimes, in fact often, these days, your sound card is built into your main board, that is, the thing inside your computer that everything else is attached to in some fashion, including your recorder. If it's not there, it's in a PCI slot on your main board someplace.

TIP

Got a mic jack? Turn off the 20dB gain boost and use that for an in, then use your headphone jack for an out.

Whatever you have will absolutely work for all purposes in this book, so long as it has a line-in jack. (And you only need that if you intend to record and restore cassettes and records.) We'll show you how to build various rigs in Chapters 7 and 8, depending on what kind of line input you've got.

2.13 Here's a pro sound card.

2.14 Here's a USB audio capture device.

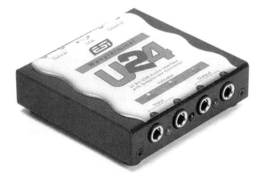

Be it known, however, that if you have an empty PCI slot (which you probably do), or an open USB port (again, you've probably got one available), you've got options. For $129, you can get a professional-quality sound card instead of a junky SoundBlaster that costs twice as much. The difference between a recording taken by your standard-issue card (usually some bastard son of a SoundBlaster, or a SoundBlaster itself) and a professional quality sound card is astounding. If you're not happy with the recordings captured by the card you already have, here are some cards and devices we recommend (again, you don't need these, but they're nice):

Killer Sound Cards for the PC

ST Audio DSP 24 Value Sound Card
www.staudio.com, $129

ESI Waveterminal 192X Sound Card
www.esi-pro.com, $299

Digital Audio Labs' CardDeluxe
www.digitalaudiolabs.com, $399

Killer Hardware for the Mac

ESI Waveterminal U24 USB Sound Card
www.esi-pro.com, $299

Preamplifiers

Say you jumped the gun a little and plugged your turntable directly into your line-in jack. You'd notice that no sound comes out of your speakers, and when you go to record, no levels are present. As you know, or could guess just by watching a turntable, an LP's grooves vibrate a stylus, and these vibrations become sound, immediately, right there. That's why you can hear a record playing even if the volume on your speakers is all the way down, though only just barely, and only if you're standing right next to your turntable.

The vibrations of the stylus then become electric signals in the head of the tone arm, and the electrical signals are passed along the tone arm, all the way on down to the tips of the RCA cables dangling from the rear of your turntable. The thing is, the vibrations in the stylus caused by the LP aren't powerful enough to be loud, and the ensuing electrical signals produced in the tone arm head are similarly weak. They must be amplified to become audible. That's the first thing a phono preamplifier does: It makes audible the relatively weak electrical audio signal coming out of your turntable.

2.15 A preamp does a couple things: first, as you may have guessed, it amplifies the signal coming from a turntable; second, it applies an equalization curve.

Now, suppose for a minute you are able to hear the record playing over your computer's speakers, even though you're not using a phono preamp. You'll be astonished at the incredible lack of bass you're hearing, and you'll wince at the overwhelming treble. That's not what records sound like, right? Well, actually, it is, up until they hit a phono preamp.

That's the second thing a preamp does: it applies what's known as an inverse RIAA Curve (yes, the very same RIAA that's suing you, as discussed in Chapter 1). It's an equalization curve—think of running a curved line through the graphic equalizer attached to your home entertainment center—that boosts bass and cuts treble. This was implemented because to cut a true bass groove in a record, you have to make the groove extremely wide—so wide, in fact, you could squeeze maybe one track onto a standard 33 1/3 RPM record. The treble comes down in order to cut what's called "surface noise," which is the high frequency sound inherent in a stylus's physical contact with the record—nails on a chalkboard, essentially.

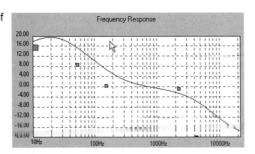

2.16 This is the inverse of the RIAA curve, the equalization curve a preamp applies to a signal.

NOTE

If it happens you're working with a record or cylinder made before 1953, and you're using a preamp that applies an RIAA Curve, playing your record or cylinder will bass you to death. This is really easy to fix. In the digital audio editing software we'll be talking about in Chapter 7, you'll often have access to a graphic equalizer. In the graphic equalizer, apply the RIAA Curve to what you record and all will be well. You're essentially reversing the RIAA Curve when you do this.

Anything with a phono-in and a line-out will work as a preamp, whether it's a plain-old stereo receiver or a mixing board. All you need to do to find out if you have a phono-in and line-out (or, sometimes, tape-out) is look at the back of any receivers or boards you have to see whether or not you've got the words "phono-in" and "line-out" (or "tape-out") written atop some red and white RCA connections.

Your stand-alone preamp choices are wide and varied, with prices ranging from $20 to $20,000. If you're looking for a decent starter kit for your PC, there's a great, inexpensive ($229) all-in-one package over at TracerTek (www.tracertek.com) that includes not only a phono preamp, but also a quality sound card, a fantastic digital audio editor, and even CD-R software. There's no comparable package for a Mac, but that's OK, because all that means is that you're set with the task of locating a decent preamp.

The only solid advice we have to offer Mac and PC users in selecting a preamp is that the digital audio-editing software packages we discuss in Chapter 7 can make up for a lot of the bad things a preamp might do, so it's not necessary to spend a lot of money here. Remember, too, that a stereo receiver will work just fine in place of a preamp, so you may not want to buy a preamp at all.

Stereo Peripherals

CD obviated records, cassette tapes, 8-tracks, reel-to-reel, and every other music-totin' medium that preceded it. That's good news here: if you don't have a turntable or a cassette deck, you can get them for next to nothing at your local pawn shop. Old stereo receivers, too, won't cost much of anything, so there's a cheap preamp for you.

In Chapter 6, we'll show you how to clean up a cassette deck, and in Chapter 7, we'll help you get your turntable in good working order.

Computer Sound Systems

We assume you have a pair of powered "multimedia" speakers attached to your machine, if not a subwoofer, or a 5.1 system. If you don't, they too range from the inexpensive to the exorbitant. All you need for this book is a pair of multimedia speakers, so you don't need to go out and purchase Cambridge SoundWorks 5.1 Dolby Digital Super MegaPackage—Labtec will do just fine.

There's one thing we need to mention here: speaker static. When you're DeHissing a tape or record, it's easy to mistake speaker static for "tape hiss." (Even when it appears on a record, it's still called "tape-hiss.") That's because they're pretty much the same thing: speaker static and tape hiss are both products of magnetism. So, see to it that you've got your speakers' knob turned down far enough to where static is inaudible when you're restoring tapes and records; otherwise you risk overapplication of the DeHiss filter—in fact, you'll be totally rid of not only hiss, but also the tune you're working on, and you'll still have hiss issuing from your speakers. We'll show you how to fiddle with your OS's audio controls such that you can turn your speakers clear way down but still have a loud signal issuing from them (see Chapter 6 and Chapter 7).

Hit Me with Those Laser Beams

You've got your gasoline, an empty bottle, and a rag. Now we're going to show you how to construct and deploy your Molotov Cocktail....

Copying Audio CDs

One of the remarkable facets of human consciousness, at least at this historical moment, is that it tends to resist change like it's the devil himself. We get used to things, grow comfortable with them, and cling to them with peculiar force. It's probably that same force we use when clinging to sanity—or life even. Our universe crumbles a bit when the liquor store runs out of our particular poison. Even if we end up with a better-quality six-pack, we'll still be bummed, simply because it's not what we're accustomed to.

We'll eagerly wager that we could get at least one analog guy—that guy who prefers his LPs to their CD equivalents—to confess that he likes his LPs not because they sound better, but rather because that vinyl sound is what he's used to, and music on vinyl constitutes his vision of what music should sound like.

This chapter will detail both the good ways and the questionable ways to duplicate an audio CD. The former because, well, we want you to have a good copy, and the latter because they illuminate problems you'll encounter in all of your audio recording endeavors.

The Order of Things

To preserve the comfortable order, we're sometimes tempted to apply old notions and familiar means to new situations, but it's often a mistake to do so. Being that many of us grew up with dual-tape decks, we might imagine that copying a CD is pretty much the same thing as duping a tape. Put the source here, put the blank there, hit the Record button, and soon enough, you've got a viable copy. Today's CD-R software can certainly emulate that procedure, and do it much faster if you have a recorder made in the last eight years. Most—in fact, let's just say all—CD-R software packages feature a copy capability and some utility or other that rips from a source drive and records to the blank in your CD-R drive with the touch of one digital Record button.

Using a copy feature, however, is not the best way to duplicate an audio CD. In fact, it ranks among the most precarious. Now, when we say "precarious," we don't mean that you'll end up with a poor copy each time you trek down this treacherous recording path. We mean that some ways are much less reliable than others. A good rule of thumb, when faced with a choice between audio CD recording procedures, is that if a procedure doesn't involve your ear, try not to have anything to do with it.

The Ubiquitous but Mainly Nefarious Copy Utility

Most of today's CD recording software packages feature a copy utility. There's usually nothing extravagant about them: many times all you get are two fields, where you select source and destination drives, and the option of involving your hard disk in the copy procedure or writing directly from one drive to another, generally known as *copying on-the-fly* (see Figure 3.1). And naturally, you'll also find some permutation of the traditional big red Record button, if not an *actual* big, red Record button. Children of the dual-tape deck generation can see where this is going already, right?

3.1 Roxio's digital version of the dual tape deck: Disc Copier, which ships with Easy CD&DVD Creator 6.

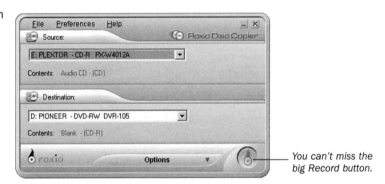

You can't miss the big Record button.

You guessed it—if you have a CD-ROM drive (or DVD-ROM drive or anything that is capable of reading CDs) and a CD-R drive, you can put whatever CD you wish to copy into a read drive and a piece of blank media into your recorder and you're halfway to a dupe. But not necessarily a good dupe, at all. Matter of fact, you might start with the dearly departed Johnny Cash and end up with at best Yoko Ono-like screeching and wailing punctuating "I Walk the Line," and at worst, wall-to-wall Yoko.

NOTE
If you have only one drive, skip to the next section, called "How Bob and Josh Copy CDs...."

To proceed with copying a CD using a copy utility, you'll need to perform Digital Audio Extraction (DAE, or as we like to say, ripping), which is more complicated than simply copying a file from a CD-ROM or DVD-ROM drive to a hard drive. After all, we're not copying files, we're copying tracks. As we've said before, digital audio data is in some respects like any other data, but there are technical differences that have a direct impact on the copying process. The complications come in how audio data is arranged on a disc and the limited directory information that tells a reader where that data is (see the sidebar "Why Is Extracting So Exacting?"). The drive containing your source disc must be DAE-capable. But don't panic. All drives shipped after 2000— that is, CD-ROM, DVD-ROM, CD-R/RW, DVD-R/RW, and so on—are capable of DAE.

Why Is Extracting So Exacting?

Given that the first CD-ROM drives weren't much more than modified audio CD players, you'd guess that CD-ROM drives would be really comfortable dealing with audio data, whether it's playback or extraction to the storage medium of your choice. That's not the case. The Red Book, the standard document that contains the published specification for Compact Disc-Digital Audio, stipulates an elegant way of writing audio data to CD, but readers of this data—stereo units, CD-ROM drives, what have you—don't need to be all that precise in the way they read.

To play an audio CD, all a CD player needs to do is get its laser somewhere near the beginning of a track, in that area of silence that precedes it. This approach is fine for playback, but for a CD-ROM drive to extract an audio track accurately and duplicate it on a hard drive in useful form, more precision is required. The reason for this is inherent in the differences between CD-Audio and CD-ROM. CD-Audio is designed for a specific purpose: linear, track-by-track playback on CD players. Because all audio discs share a simple structure that is not common to all CD-ROMs, an audio disc contains less information to describe the organization of its contents than a CD-ROM, which may contain any kind of data used on a computer.

continued

An audio disc's table of contents (TOC), much like a book's, is a good general resource for knowing what's where, but it won't always lead you to the right spot. Although this book's table of contents may tell you on what page the chapter "Copying Audio CDs" begins, that doesn't tell you where the part about audio extraction is. Likewise, the TOC on an audio CD tells the CD reader about where the song starts, but unlike a CD-ROM with data on it, it does not tell it exactly where it starts.

Audio discs were designed to be read sequentially, in real time, with the digital data converted to an analog signal that would be played through a stereo's speakers. There was no need to have data on the disc to pinpoint the exact location of the beginning of a song.

That extra data containing an exact starting address for each song takes up space that could otherwise be used for storing more music. The 2,048 bytes of user data in each 2,352-byte CD-ROM sector can be accessed exactly because the header information in each sector contains the precise address of the data block.

An audio block, on the other hand, contains 2,352 bytes in each physical block, and all of these bytes are used for audio data. No header exists; there is no information in the block that allows for the exact positioning of the read head over a specific block.

After making sure our hardware is equipped to rip, we'll fire up the software and get down to business. We'll be working with a Plextor PX-W4012A (a CD-R/RW drive) and a Pioneer DVR-105 (a DVD-R/RW drive). Both drives record CDs, so we could use either as the source drive. However, we'll use the Plextor drive, because it's the faster reader. (You'll see why this is important in a moment.)

NOTE

Both of the drives used in this example are also capable of DAE, so we could risk an on-the-fly copy. If we were to run an on-the-fly copy, it would be purely for illustrative purposes: we highly recommend against on-the-fly duping for a number of reasons, but, we ain't the boss of you, or anybody else for that matter, as we find bosses morally and ethically objectionable.

If you happen to be a boss, fear the revolution, you bourgeois pig.

Let's now get started on copying the CD:

1. Fire up the copy utility software program of your choice—for this example, we'll use Nero 6 (www.nero.com).

2. From the scrolling pane off to the left, select CD Copy. Four tabs appear: Image, Copy Options, Read Options, and Burn. Click the Copy Options tab (see Figure 3.2). There you'll see a check box next to those three dreaded words: On the fly.

3.2 The Nero 6 copy utility should look familiar to anyone who has used a disc-copy utility before. The Copy Options tab offers you several choices before you start copying your audio CD. Here, for illustrative purposes only, we've checked the On the Fly box.

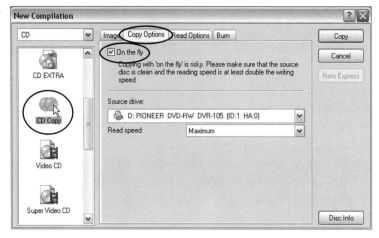

You have two options: you can check the box or leave it alone. Our advice? Leave it alone—don't copy audio CDs on-the-fly.

If you do check that box, you'll notice even the horrible tyrant Nero tells you not to copy on-the-fly (see Figure 3.2). The upside, however, is that the copy procedure will move much more quickly. If you do proceed here, contravening Nero's advice, you'll risk encountering weird stuff such as buffer underruns and buffer overflow (see Chapter 2, "Hardware and Software," for more information). With the advent of technologies such as BURNProof and JustLink, buffer underruns and overflows aren't the horror they used to be, so you won't necessarily end up with a ruined piece of media. You may, however, end up with a bunch of nasty little digital bleeps, blips, and other assorted digital artifacts on your freshly recorded disc. And if you're working with an older drive or a drive lacking some form of buffer underrun protection, you're out of luck.

NOTE

Okay, alright, he admits it: Bob, during times of weakness, copies on-the-fly. If his recording sucks, he just pitches the disc. Josh, on the other hand, hates to see media wasted and has learned infinite patience from his studies in Tibet, so he never, ever copies on-the-fly. Josh admits he's horribly jealous when Bob's recordings come out okay, even despite his Buddhistic composure. When Bob's discs are bad, though, Josh gets the last laugh, and he laughs the laugh of 1,000 demons feasting on the soul of a damned wretch.

3. In a hurry to copy your CD? All you have to do now is click the Burn tab, configure as you see fit (select your speed, enable your buffer underrun protection, and so on), click Copy in the upper-right corner (see Figure 3.3), and you're finished. But if you want to learn a little more about the additional choices you have for copying your audio CD, read on. Then pick up with step 4.

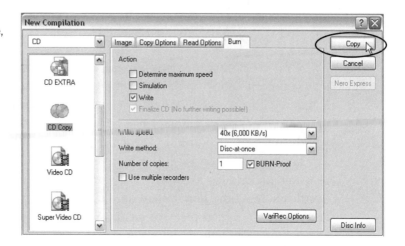

If data isn't arriving fast enough to keep up with the recorder, it may spell doom for your poor piece of media. CD recording requires a constant flow of data, so a recorder keeps a reservoir of data for itself—a buffer—so that little flow interruptions, diversions, and occasional jostling that occur in typical data transfer don't mess everything up. The recorder can then proceed writing data from the buffer, which will gradually fill itself up again.

Sometimes, though, interruptions in the data stream are so severe that the buffer empties out, the data flow stops, and recording grinds to a halt. This is called *buffer underrun*, and can happen for several reasons, but often it's because your source drive reads too slowly and cannot keep up with the writing process. Unless your drive features a buffer underrun prevention technology, this would result in what's known as a "coaster," a CD that won't play, but will serve to protect the varnish on a coffee table from beverage condensation.

Audio discs can have unreadable areas on them, resulting from a scratch or dirt, or because the CD itself was poorly pressed. During playback, the unreadable areas, called *errors*, don't really pose a problem: CD players by nature go back and take another stab and are usually able to read the data they couldn't read the first time. That's called *error correction*. Readers normally don't correct for errors during on-the-fly copying because that takes time they don't really have here. When a reader encounters errors during an on-the-fly copy, it may stop offering data altogether; the software won't attempt to compensate, and you'll get a buffer underrun. Many CD recording programs—or even the drives themselves in some cases—will throw up their arms in exasperation at this error and pass on whatever they feel like making up that day to placate the recorder. What they pass on ain't Barry Manilow. Other software will send a string of 0s (essentially digital silence) to the recorder until it starts receiving decent data again.

NOTE

The other main cause of buffer underruns is too many other applications hogging the PC, especially on slower and RAM-deprived systems. Try to avoid running other programs during burning, especially on-the-fly dupes.

Should your recorder feature one, this cessation of data flow invokes whatever buffer underrun protection scheme it's got (BURNProof, JustLink, and so on). The laser in your drive simply stops writing until the buffer fills up again, then returns to within nanometers of where it stopped. There it resumes normal writing. Nanometers, though, are kind of a thing when we're talking about CD data structure: nanometers might mean a digital artifact, bleeps and such, during playback.

Too much data may arrive in the CD-ROM's memory cache during an on-the-fly copy, which happens when the ROM drive is reading the audio disc faster than the data is being asked for by your software and the recorder. Since the CD-ROM drive has to be on its toes, it might start forgetting older data to handle new data, the data being read. That's *buffer overflow*. Your software might inquire about this forgotten information, because it hasn't been written yet, and the CD-ROM drive only kind of remembers where it was due to the imprecise nature of digital audio. So, imprecisely, it reads and passes on imprecise information. Although you probably won't blow the disc entirely, you'll get some very unpleasant noise. This happens rarely these days, but it underscores the value of the buffer.

Fortunately, you can overcome most of those problems by removing that check from the small box that tells Nero to copy on-the-fly (see Figure 3.4). Nero, along with all of today's other CD-R software packages, will create what's known as an image, a kind of utopian data layout, on your hard disk and then take that layout and burn it to CD.

3.4 Removing the check from the On the Fly box increases your chances of a successful copy.

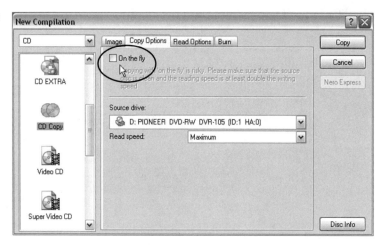

Another bonus: when you burn an image, most programs give you the opportunity to save that image. In Nero, you do this by clicking on the Image tab, removing the check from Delete Image File After Disc Copy, selecting a directory for your image, and then naming it (see Figure 3.5). This enables you to make multiple copies from that image, so you'll never have to bother extracting your disc again. Bear in mind, though, that these image files occupy a lot of hard disk space (even more than 700MB for a full disc), so keep an eye on your resources if you've got a bunch of images laying around.

3.5 Leaving the image on your hard disk does two things: it enables you to make multiple copies of the same CD at different times, and it takes up a lot of space.

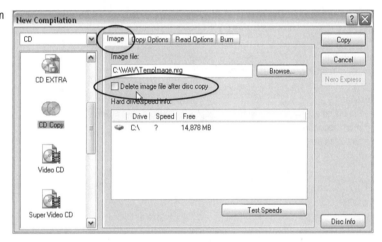

The cool thing about hard disks is that, unlike CD-R drives, they can deal with interruptions. So, the process of extracting data to a hard disk and burning an image to CD is much more reliable than the on-the-fly process, and the ripping process can hit all sorts of minor snags without impairing or stopping the data extraction and transfer. Time ceases to be a concern here for your software and your source drive: your software won't have to answer to a recorder just yet, and the demands your software makes on your source drive won't be so stringent. Most important, there's time to get data right during the transfer to hard disk—the CD-ROM drive can have another go at the data if it needs to when it encounters an error. Everything relaxes a bit, you know, like when the bosses leave to go play golf, or whatever it is they do when they're not exploiting the masses. What's more, when it comes time to burn the data, the machinations of the rip are behind you, and you're left with a straightforward data transfer from a source (the hard drive) that won't stop and sputters like a drive trying to read and rip a timeworn source CD.

So let's proceed:

4. Click on the Burn tab in Nero, or whatever copy utility program you're using. The on-the-fly check box back under the Copy Options tab isn't checked, so now we need to make a few more decisions.

First, since we're being safe here, we can tell our recorder to record at maximum speed in the Speed field (see Figure 3.6). If we were doing an on-the-fly copy, we might have to take our recorder speed all the way on down to 1x, depending on how quickly our CD-ROM drive is capable of extracting audio. (Remember that our source drive must extract faster than the data is being written, but not too much faster.)

3.6 Because burning from an image is relatively safe, you can record at what's known as "Ramming Speed," that is, the maximum recording speed your drive is capable of.

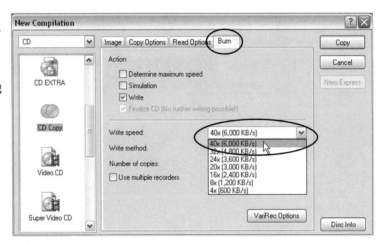

Second, we'll tell Nero how many copies of the source CD we want—we just want one today, but you're totally welcome to make more than that (see Figure 3.7). Keep in mind that Nero will burn to multiple drives simultaneously if you want it to, but that's a strange and unreliable practice that requires at minimum multiple identical recorders. Multiple copies, in this case, refers to successive burns to the same drive.

3.7 Just one copy today, thanks.

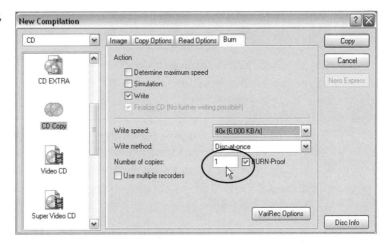

Third and finally, we're given the option of simulating the burn before we commit, just burning, or both. Simulation will run the copy procedure without actually writing anything to CD-R and will report any problems encountered. Selecting Write will simply go ahead with the burn. Both of us are in a hurry today, so we're going to record by selecting Write, all by itself (see Figure 3.8).

3.8 We're in a hurry, so we're selecting only Write under the Burn tab. Note, too, that we enabled BurnProof. Were we dauntless men, we might disable it, just to see what happens. (Odds are good you'll get a coaster, but coasters make nice Christmas tree ornaments in addition to their other functions.)

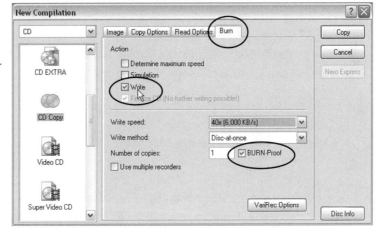

5. Click Copy in the upper-right corner of the window, as before, and begin the waiting process.

Depending on the extraction speed of your source drive, and the speed of your recorder, you'll be waiting 10 minutes to an hour, but eventually you'll have a copy.

When you finally have a copy to listen to, you may find it stinks. The possible reasons for its stinkiness are numerous and extraordinarily difficult to pinpoint, but know this: That's not the first time that's happened, and that's why we do things differently around here. And we do them with only one drive.

How Bob and Josh Copy CDs (Most of the Time), a Handy Tip, and Something We Bet You Didn't Know

We didn't listen to the tracks that hit the hard disk before we burned them to disc, so if our copy stinks, we don't know if the problem arose from the extraction process or the recording process. Not only that, every single song on that CD is on its duplicate. What if we don't particularly like some of those songs? We're stuck there, too. And if we don't particularly like the job the studio did in producing and engineering this artist's work—why is that bass so muffled?—we didn't have an opportunity to adjust for the perceived faults using our digital audio editing software. So this copy utility, prone to error already, has also deprived us of any flexibility. That's why we prefer to extract to hard disk, listen to the tracks, work our magic on them as needed, and *then* burn them. That solves everything—almost, anyway.

NOTE This procedure involves, above all, patience. If you don't have any, go ahead and use one of the procedures described earlier to copy your audio CDs.

Here, we're going to use Audio CD Ripper, an extraction utility we snagged for free from www.download.com (see Figure 3.9). (Download.com has all kinds of freeware over there for both Mac and PC—have a look.) We'll first extract each track to a folder we've dedicated to digital audio on the hard disk. After that, we'll listen to each track over our computer speakers or headphones, paying close attention to the quality of the ripped tracks. (You can listen to these tracks with any audio playback software you've got, and you've got it, whether or not you know it.)

3.9 Audio CD Ripper is a good, simple, and—best of all—free digital audio extraction tool for the PC.

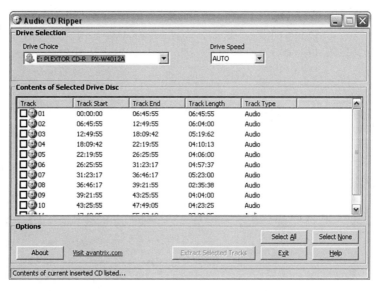

1. The first thing to do, of course, is put a CD in your CD-R/RW, CD-ROM, DVD-ROM, or whatever drive you've found extracts audio best. If you don't have a CD, borrow one from your son, daughter, niece, nephew, grandson, granddaughter, grandniece, grandnephew, or neighbor.

TIP

Should you find yourself borrowing a CD or purchasing one for the first time, it's been our experience that Brian Setzer crosses all age and taste boundaries. Josh's dearly departed grandmother loved Setzer: "That's the way guitar should be played," she said. She also said, "Josh, I don't know where you got it, but you've got 'kitchen sense,'" which he thinks means that either a) Josh is a good cook, or b) Josh knows better than to enter a kitchen. So if you see a Stray Cats CD, a Brian Setzer Orchestra CD, or a Brian Setzer CD, go for that.

2. On some machines, your CD will begin playing over your speakers automatically. Make whatever's playing it stop playing it, and shut that program down for now. You can return to it later when you're performing quality assurance testing on your tracks.

3. Next, open Audio CD Ripper, or the extraction tool of your choice.

4. In Audio CD Ripper, choose the drive containing your CD from the Drive Choice drop-down menu. (We're going with the Plextor here, see Figure 3.10.) Your tracks will appear in the scrolling Contents of Selected Drive Disc pane.

3.10 We're selecting our source drive here, which contains the CD we want to copy.

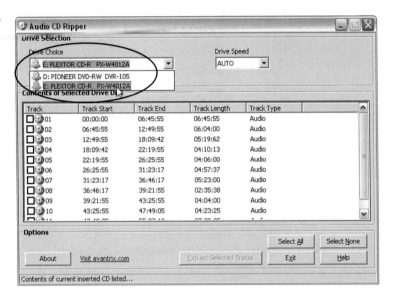

5. Since we're assuming you intend to copy the entire source CD, we're going to click the Select All button in the lower-right corner (see Figure 3.11), which will add a check mark to every box adjacent to the tracks in the Contents of Selected Drive pane. We'll then click Extract Selected Tracks, right there next to the Select All button.

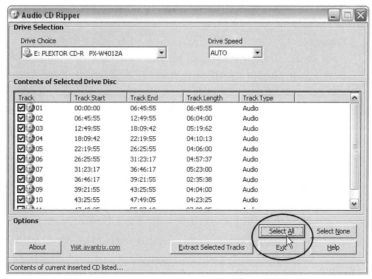

3.11 Click on Select All if you intend to copy your entire CD to your hard disk for later listening and burning.

6. When you click Extract Selected Tracks in step 5, up pops another window, Extraction Options (see Figure 3.12), where you're presented with a few options. Browse on over to the folder you want to put your tracks in—this by clicking on the folder icon button next to the field beneath Extraction Folder—and then choose a name for your tracks in the Track Naming field. (We just go with the default "Track," because we've got the source CD jewel case sitting right here and can refer to it for track names, album name, and so on.)

3.12 Extraction Options enables you to specify a directory for your tracks and a naming convention. Defaults are fine, but do make sure you know where your tracks are going.

7. Under MP3 Options, make sure the box next to Encode Extracted Tracks to MP3 Format is *not* checked (see Figure 3.13). (We'll talk all about MP3s—what they are, how to create them, and how to "decode" them such that they conform with the CD Audio standard—in Chapter 4, "Recording MP3s to CD.") Here we want true, pure, Red Book tracks, not MP3s.

3.13 Don't check the Encode Extracted Tracks to MP3 Format. If there's a check there, remove it, because it will add unnecessary compression and an extra decompression stage to the burn.

8. All you have to do now is click the good old OK button. Soon, all your tracks will arrive in the destination folder you specified.

9. What's left now is to listen to your extracted tracks. If you find you have an ugly track, simply go back to Audio CD Ripper, click Select None, select only that track by putting a check next to it in the Contents of Selected Drive pane, and then repeat the entire procedure described in steps 1-8 (see Figure 3.14).

3.14 You can select tracks one by one in Audio CD Ripper by simply checking the boxes next to the ones you want.

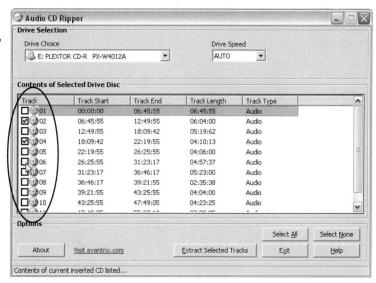

If that doesn't do the trick, return once again to Audio CD Ripper, and select the track. From the Drive Speed drop-down menu—located next to the Drive Choice drop-down—choose a "low" speed (see Figure 3.15).

The Plextor reads on up to 40x, so if we encounter a problem, we'll take the read speed on down to 20x, and then go ahead with extraction. If that doesn't fix the problem, we'll take the speed to 12x, extract, and on and on until we reach 1x. If 1x doesn't work, take your drive to wherever you bought it and throw it at the person who sold it to you— point being, lower read speeds produce better results, simply because there's ample time for reading. It's like the boss'll be out for weeks with a killer flu from his "business trip" to Taiwan *and* it's casual Friday *and* Jerry from Accounting just found the stash left over from the Holiday Party *and* you're actually finished with the report you've been pretending to be working on for the last month or so.

3.15 Extracting at lower speeds will probably fix whatever ails you.

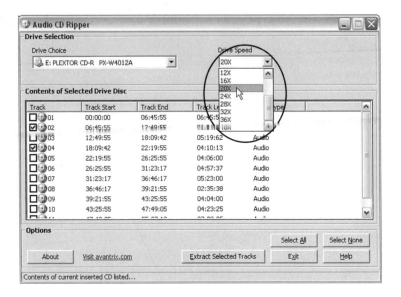

TIP

Here's that tip we mentioned earlier: if you've got a store-bought CD that skips or is otherwise malfunctioning, extract the whole thing at a low speed, as we just mentioned, and burn it. The ensuing copy most likely won't skip or otherwise malfunction anymore (and the copy you make is actually of better logical quality than the store-bought pressed CD [that, incidentally is the thing we bet you didn't know]).

The Burn

The only thing to mention here is that we left both the leading and trailing silences on the tracks in the previous steps, so we're going to do a disc-at-once burn. A reminder: Not all drives support disc-at-once, so be sure to check your drive—your software will usually tell you—before you decide to leave leading and trailing silences tacked on to your tracks.

Queue 'em up and burn 'em, just exactly as we showed you in Chapter 1, "Diving Right In," using whatever CD recording software you've got laying around. Just so you know, this particular copy of this CD will be going into Josh's car, so the next time his car gets broken into, he won't be out the fifteen bucks it costs to replace his store-bought copy. Better than a car alarm, we tell you, these CD-R drives. Cheaper, too.

CHAPTER

4

Recording MP3s to CD

It's Chapter 4—do you know where your children are? They're probably downloading MP3s from Kazaa! Stop them! They're destroying the record industry! God help us all!

We're going to assume you know what an MP3 is, in its "music you download from the Internet" sense. We don't read *The New York Times* every day, but the days we have, there's typically some mention of MP3 in it, if not on the front page. We're now also seeing TV commercials with lawsuit victims touting Apple's MP3 download service, iTunes. Just today, we saw a RICO countersuit lodged against the RIAA (the Recording Industry Association of America, which is, among other things, the litigating arm of the recording industry) for its $40 million (give or take) lawsuit against yet another single mother whose child downloaded MP3s. Find out more about the RIAA at www.riaa.com.

NOTE

RICO, in case you don't watch *The Sopranos*, stands for Racketeer Influenced and Corrupt Organizations. Congress passed the RICO Act in 1970 to destroy organized crime, which, at the time, was a very significant economic factor. These days, you see it used in other contexts: DOJ and DA suits against corporate and other terrorist organizations, mainly. (For more info, check out this unbelievably long URL: **http://usinfo.state.gov/usa/infousa/laws/majorlaw/rico/rico.htm**.)

We're also going to assume that you have access to the knowledge required to download an MP3. If you don't know how to procure an MP3, almost everyone from the pre-adolescent through the elderly demographic will be able to furnish you with instructions. If you're still having problems, Google it (www.google.com). This chapter will concern itself not with how to get MP3s, but rather how to prepare the MP3s you already have to be burned to CD.

Both of us have very strong feelings regarding the politics, litigation, and general furor surrounding MP3, but we're going to resist the temptation to op-ed here and instead tell you what MP3 is and isn't, show you how to "decode" MP3 files such that they may be burned to CD, and offer a couple of tips and tricks when working with them. If you want to know what we think of the RIAA, MP3, and so on, we'd again have you Google it. You may even be able to find that ancient text about what happened when Josh called Hilary Rosen—then-president and CEO of the RIAA—"stupid."

Things You Should Know About MP3 and File Sharing

First and foremost, MP3 in and of itself is not illegal. If you have a track and you want to make an MP3 out of it, go ahead; that's fine, you're still a good citizen. If you're a band and wish to post MP3s of a couple cuts to the Internet to put hooks in our mouths, that's perfectly legal as well. You could even post the whole album, if you want. It's also perfectly legal for anyone to download the MP3s posted by your band, so long as you provide your consent.

Is File Sharing Illegal?

The answer is no, not intrinsically.

In a landmark decision—Sony Corp. v. Universal City Studios, usually referred to as "The Betamax Case"—the U.S. Supreme Court ruled, essentially, that it's okay to "time-shift" TV shows by recording them to watch at a later time (that is, you can set your Betamax, or VCR, or whatever to record *Passions*—Josh's favorite soap—when you know you'll be at work). The Supreme Court's decision states, "The sale of copying equipment, like the sale of other articles of commerce, does not constitute contributory [copyright] infringement if the product is widely used for legitimate, unobjectionable purposes. Indeed, it need merely be capable of substantial noninfringing uses."

That last sentence is of tremendous importance: "substantial noninfringing uses" means that anything that can be used for a lot of legitimate purposes—getting a thesis to your professor by way of peer-to-peer file sharing rather than downloading something copyrighted, for example, or, allegorically, using your microwave to cook things rather than hitting someone over the head with it—can't automatically be taken off the market, or closed in cyberspace. You have to prove in a court of law that something doesn't have "substantial noninfringing uses" in order to kill it or shut it down.

The U.S. Supreme Court continued, quoting the District Court where all this business started, "Whatever the future percentage of legal versus illegal home-use recording might be, an injunction which seeks to deprive the public of the very tool or article of commerce capable of some noninfringing use would be an extremely harsh remedy, as well as one unprecedented in copyright law."

continues

continued

The RIAA would have you believe the law that applies here is a piece of legislation passed in 1998 called the Digital Millennium Copyright Act (DMCA). Written largely to update copyright law to encompass the Internet and delineate the responsibilities and liabilities of online service providers vis a vis potentially copyright-infringing uses of their servers to post and distribute information, the DMCA predates peer-to-peer file sharing and consequently says nothing about it. The RIAA has nonetheless persisted in an aggressive reading of the DMCA, arguing that it somehow grandfathers in P2P technology that it neither addresses nor anticipates. In a December 2003 U.S. Federal Appeals court ruling, the presiding judge nailed them for just such a misreading, so what did they do? They went back in January and had the DMCA amended to support their position on P2P file sharing so they could continue to "protect" artists from their fans by prosecuting them.

We believe, and would argue that the ruling in the Betamax case, protecting technologies with "substantial non-infringing uses," applies to file-sharing software, and that no amount of retrofitting the DMCA will legitimize the RIAA's witchhunt. Either way, the blessed forward-thinking programmers will figure out a way around everything, so we'd advise the RIAA, Metallica, et al., to stop with the litigation already, and work with us instead. Seriously, your future is at stake.

We're starting to get a bit off track now, so if you want more information, check out http://www.virtualrecordings.com/betamax.htm and http://www.copyright.gov/legislation/dmca.pdf.

Second, MP3 is what's known as a "lossy" compression scheme. (See the section called "What Is MP3 Really?" for further details.) You'll notice that a typical MP3 occupies about 3-5 megabytes (MB) of disk space, whereas its CD counterpart—that is, the track ripped from CD that became this MP3— weighs in at a whopping 36-60 MB. That's because MP3 compression removes and destroys audio information irretrievably (but in such a way that the track still sounds good). Given that, ask yourself: do I want to pay 99 cents for something that has been stripped of all that information? In other words, would I pay $42,000 for the chassis of a 2002 Mercedes SLK, or $1.29 for an empty bottle of Pepsi?

NOTE PepsiCo, Inc., if you haven't seen the commercial, is colluding with Mac to promote iTunes and its own "sweet snot." (Josh's high-school chemistry/physics teacher gave that sobriquet to Pepsi—hi, Mr. Hanks, by the way. Bet you never guessed you and Josh would be colleagues, huh?)

Third, record companies make a huge profits. Ask yourself: who is the thief here, the record company relaxing atop its pile of ill-gotten gold or the honor student who downloads an MP3? Is it theft to take what's already stolen? For fun, let's take a closer look here at how the system works. When a band gets a contract, they sign papers and receive a chunk of change (sometimes in the millions). That money is a small percentage of what the record company bets the album will make on the market. The record company, of course, keeps the rest of the proceeds from the sales of that album (and spends another tiny little bit for promotion—greasing palms at MTV, sticking $100 bills into jewel cases headed to KRUD, and so on).

Now, if the profit from the album exceeds the record company's bet, they then pay to the artist(s) what's called a "royalty." Hardly any band receives royalties, but the record company still makes a huge profit. Now, knowing that the artists have already been paid and in all likelihood shall make nothing further (at least for that album), do you still feel guilty about downloading a free MP3? You're certainly not hurting them in the way the RIAA suggests.

What Moby Thinks

The following quote is from a piece in *The New York Times* (9/14/03) called "File-Sharing Battle Leaves Musicians Caught in the Middle," written by Neil Strauss:

Moby sez: "How can a 14-year-old who has an allowance of $5 a week feel bad about downloading music produced by multimillionaire musicians and greedy record companies…The record companies should approach that 14-year-old and say: 'Hey, it's great that you love music. Instead of downloading music for free, why don't you try this very inexpensive service that will enable you to listen to a lot of music and also have access to unreleased tracks and ticket discounts and free merchandise?'"

Fourth, we inhabit an economy on the verge of depression, and have for the last five years or so. Ask yourself: can we really blame MP3 for a decline in record sales, given that we have a choice between food and Eminem's latest sexist, homophobic, culture-robbing blather?

Fifthly, and finally, Josh freely admits he has hundreds, if not thousands of MP3s he didn't pay for, and will not refer to them as "stolen," but rather "liberated" (and has bought entire albums based upon what he sampled, MP3-wise). Thus far, he has eluded the cold, clammy clutches of the RIAA for a couple reasons:

1. He's a scientist and, consequently, must do research.

2. Justice has a name, and it is Bob Starrett, Juris Doctor.

   Josh has a rap sheet long as the Mississippi, but replace the words "a bridesmaid" and "a bride" in the old saying "always a bridesmaid, never a bride" with the words "indicted" and "convicted," and you'll get an idea of Bob's legal prowess.

NOTE

Seriously, Josh does have "research" as his defense, should he end up facing the RIAA in court, and many of you probably don't. (You do have a doctrine called "Fair Use" that you may summon as a defense, though.) Do be careful, unless you go in for the idea that private property ought to be abolished—as Josh does—and do be prepared to face the consequences.

Come to think of it, should you wish to file a class action suit against the RIAA—California would probably be the place to do it—get a good and willing attorney, then have her or his firm ring us up. We'll gladly do anything within our power to help.

What Is MP3 Really?

There are sounds we, with our specific biological makeup, never hear. If suddenly we were able to hear all the things around us, the world would become pretty cacophonous—so cacophonous, in fact, we'd probably go insane. Every time you spoke with your neighbor, you might hear every single projectile particle of saliva crash against the roof of his mouth, and likely your face, too, if he's a spitter. A sneeze could sound like the Fourth of July. And listening to Charlie Parker, you'd hear, in addition to every note he played, the rush of breath producing the note.

These sounds we never perceive do cause mechanical responses in your ear—the fibers in your cochlea vibrate with the stimuli, and the whole sonic picture is there, breath, spit, and all. There is a moment, though, before conscious perception, when your brain processes the whole sonic picture and filters out a great deal of stuff. Your brain then passes on a signal mainly devoid of breath and spit to your consciousness: a second moment of hearing, as it were, the auditory experience we know as genuine human hearing. This is why you don't hear Bird's breath, or so much of it anyway.

A theory, like this one, of the way hearing works is known as a *psycho-acoustic model.* You'll often hear that tiny phrase invoked in conjunction with MP3. When a model like this is applied to digital material with the aim of compressing the material, it's called *perceptual coding,* meaning simply compression, or coding, according to the way human senses are thought by science to work.

MP3 Encoding

MP3 encoding works basically by emulating your brain in the process we just described, or at least by beating your brain to the sonic punch. The encoding process removes the sonic information your brain would have filtered out if the nonencoded sample were hitting your ear, thus reducing the amount of information in a sample and subsequently reducing the amount of space a sample occupies on your hard disk.

Speculation and empirical evidence suggest that one of the things your brain filters out is a weak signal directly next to a strong signal. Imagine Bird blowing through his saxophone—just blowing, producing no note. You can hear that, right? Now imagine him blowing a note. Though that blowing you could hear before remains—albeit in a different form—it's barely detectable, if at all, beside the note he's blowing. Your brain admits the strong note Bird produces into conscious perception but censors his relatively weak breath, though his breath is distinctly there, producing the note. This filtering is known as *signal masking, frequency masking,* or *auditory masking.* MP3 encoding is sound discriminating in much the manner of the human ear, removing the digital information that comprises these weak signals and leaving the strong signals in place.

MP3 also removes low-amplitude sonic information all the way across the frequency spectrum, that is, sounds that are there, bass through treble, but sounds we don't hear, again by nature of the way we're built. These occur below what's known as the *minimal audition threshold.* A nice mathematical curve describes this threshold, making it easy on encoding software developers.

An MP3 encoder does one last thing: Huffman coding. Say you wrote an important letter that's three-and-a-half pages long, but you're broke and have only one stamp and can therefore send just three pages. You get it in your head that if you turn the phrase "Would that it were, dearest sweetest belovedest," which occurs commonly in your letter, into simply "01" you could save a lot of space. Then, you see that if you turn your oft-repeated "beware that infernal Goya" into "11" you could save even more space. After that, you see that, though you only say it a handful of times, by reducing the epithet "stinking swine" to "0011," you could compress it further still. Pretty soon, you've gone through your whole letter, which now reads something like 010101010110011 and is 20 percent thinner. So lick your one remaining stamp and fire that bad boy off.

That's pretty much what Huffman coding does. It goes through the data produced by the first part of MP3 encoding, finds commonly occurring stuff and assigns it a small tag, then finds less common stuff and assigns it a larger tag, then finds even less common stuff and assigns it an even larger tag, and so on. It's not much different from a video compression scheme that identifies common visual elements between frames, such as the background behind a talking head, and gives it a single value to exploit its redundancy and reduce the video's typically cumbersome file size.

So that's how MP3 encoding works. The Fraunhofer Institute (http://www.fraunhofer.de/english/) started working on this in 1987, with the goal of satisfying the requirements of a digital broadcast project—they probably had no idea that this way of encoding would come to rule the Internet and perhaps didn't even see the Internet explosion on the horizon.

In 1989, the Moving Picture Experts Group (MPEG, www.mpeg.org)—a subgroup of the International Standards Organization (ISO), which produces standards for both the digital and nondigital world—was charged with finding somewhere in the world a way to compress digital audio and visual content for storage as well as the accompanying way to decode this information for playback. The call for proposals went out. The Fraunhofer Institute's idea was declared the winner in 1992, and its way of encoding and decoding (well, sort of anyway) came to be designated MPEG-1, and was adopted as a standard. MPEG-1 came in three flavors: MPEG-1, Layer 1; MPEG-1, Layer 2; and MPEG-1, Layer 3.

MPEG-1, Layer 3, is particularly cool where audio compression is concerned: you can get a super-small file with super-high quality, whereas the other layers produce files of similar quality but of larger size. Perfect for the Internet, right? Files compressed according to the MPEG-1, Layer 3, scheme have ".MP3" as an extension, and since "MP3" is by a long shot easier to utter than "MPEG-1, Layer 3," these files came to be referred to as "MP3s."

That's the long and short of it.

The Easy Way to Record MP3s to CD (a.k.a., Bob's Way)

Three, maybe four years ago, CD-R software manufacturers took notice of this MP3 phenomenon sweeping the nation and began to include MP3-related functions in their programs. Today, CD-R software is virtually built around MP3 and audio CD. With your CD-R software bundle, you get players; playlist editors; automated decoding; media "search" utilities that'll locate all your MP3s, WAVs, and AIFFs for you; and on and on and on. They've even co-opted the "skin," this magical thing originating with early stand-alone MP3 players that enables you to change the look and feel of your software's interface.

A good example of this is Audio Central (see Figure 4.1), part of Roxio's ubiquitous Easy CD & DVD Creator 6 (www.roxio.com). We'll use Audio Central on a PC here to illustrate how easy it is now to make a full-fledged, Red Book audio CD out of MP3s.

4.1 Audio Central is a perfect example of how CD-R software manufacturers have striven to accommodate audio recording.

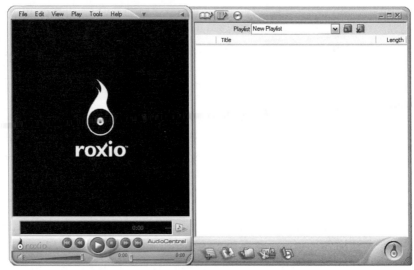

If you happen to open Audio Central via Windows' Start menu, you'll notice it's in a subdirectory full of other audio-related stuff (see Figure 4.2), whereas everything else sits in plain sight in the main directory. Relative to the short history of CD, this is a very recent phenomenon: it used to be, not more than four years ago, that you'd find audio CD among all the other types of CD (CD-ROM, VCD, and so on)—and possibly as the virtually unrecognizable CD-DA—when you were preparing a layout. Now it's up top, bold and highlighted, flanked by all sorts of other audio-related tools. Don't quote us or anything, but we're guessing that's because recording audio CDs is a popular activity among people who own recorders.

4.2 Look at all that audio stuff!

1. The first thing you'll want to do is compile a playlist, which will become your audio CD when we're all done here. (We're using Audio Central.) You do this by first choosing File > Open (see Figure 4.3). In the window that appears, navigate to the folder containing your MP3s.

4.3 This is the beginning of most MP3-to-CD projects: creating a playlist.

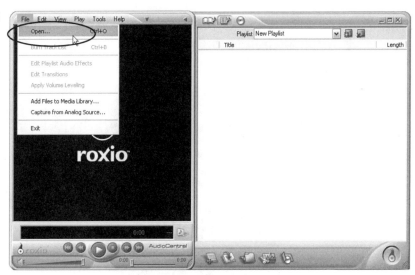

2. Once there, pick out a handful of MP3s you want to burn to CD by holding down the Ctrl button and left-clicking your tunes (see Figure 4.4). Shortly, they'll appear in the Playlist pane, and begin playing. Stop them.

4.4 Holding down the Ctrl button on your keyboard enables you to select multiple items, whether they're audio files or Word documents. Do only MP3s for now; Word files don't sound so good when burned to an audio CD.

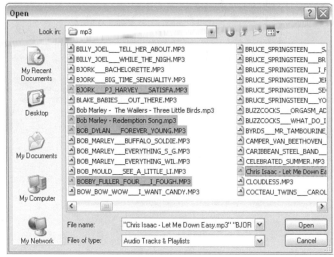

3. Right-click anywhere on your playlist. Choose Apply Volume Leveling from the menu that appears (see Figure 4.5). What that does is brings all your tracks to the same relative "loudness." (Technically speaking, this is called gain normalization, which you'll see us do a lot of in this book, most especially in Chapter 8, "Polishing Your Compilation Disc.")

4.5 Volume leveling is a weird, proprietary way to say "gain normalization." Normalization, in a nutshell, is the process of bringing everything up to a standard loudness relative to 11 on Spinal Tap's Marshall Amp.

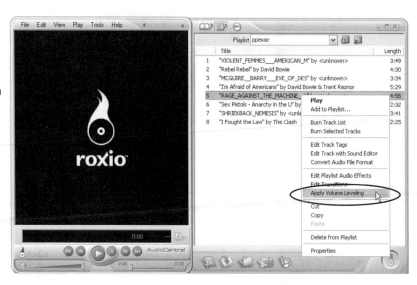

4. Click OK after you see the window mentioning that the volume leveling might take a second. You'll get a progress meter after that (see Figure 4.6); it'll take maybe a minute to get these eight tracks "volume leveled."

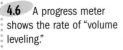

4.6 A progress meter shows the rate of "volume leveling."

5. Now click the big Record button in the lower-right corner.

A new window called Burn Setup should pop up. (Okay, this is getting strange: first "Apply Volume Leveling," then "Redbook"? Roxio should know better than anyone that it's "Red Book," this being the sixth iteration of Easy CD Creator and all.)

6. Here, choose Normal Audio CD (Redbook) from the drop-down menu in the Disc Format area, choose your recorder from the Destination drop-down menu, choose your write speed, and select the Disc-At-Once radio button. You can see our whole configuration in Figure 4.7.

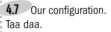

4.7 Our configuration. Taa daa.

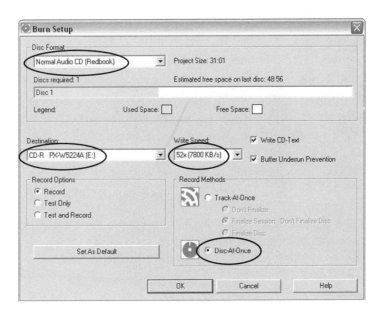

7. Click OK. Audio Central will keep you apprised of how things are going in the Burn Progress window. You'll shortly have a standard audio CD.

That's it, but if you ask Josh, he'll tell you there's a better way....

The Slightly Less Easy but, in Josh's Opinion, Better Way to Burn MP3s to CD

Here's where Josh says to Bob, "You fool! You've deprived yourself of flexibility!" and Bob responds not with words, but rather with the cruddy CD he just burned, hurling it directly at Josh's jugular vein. Josh ducks, evading Bob's makeshift shuriken, and retaliates with the microwave mentioned in the sidebar "Is File Sharing Illegal?" earlier in this chapter. Very common occurrence at the lab here, but remember, microwaves have substantial noninfringing uses, as do CD recorders, MP3s, and CD-R media.

You've got MP3s, you turned them into an audio CD, isn't that good enough? No, it's not, according to Josh. Josh insists on seeing and listening to the WAVs or AIFFs produced by MP3 decoding.

NOTE "Decoding" is a misnomer, by the way, as is "decompressing." You don't get any sonic information back when you transform an MP3 into a WAV or AIFF, you get filler, like styrofoam packing peanuts without the deleterious environmental consequences.

Audio Central automatically turns your MP3s into standard audio CD tracks and burns them without your getting to see or listen to the standard audio CD track. That's a problem. What if the decoder messes up and makes The Fly out of Vincent Price (or worse, Jeff Goldblum)? What if you want to cross-fade a couple tracks? What if there's not enough bass for your taste? That's why Josh insists on seeing and hearing the WAVs and AIFFs resulting from the decoding process before he commits them to disc.

NOTE See Chapter 8 for instructions on how to do crossfades, equalization, gain normalization, and all that fun stuff.

Let's then manually decode a few MP3s, so that we may at the very least hear what we're burning, if not haul off and alter them somehow.

1. Download Winamp from www.winamp.com. (It don't cost nothin'—see Figure 4.8.) Do a full install.

4.8 Winamp, long a staple of MP3heads' arsenals, remains freeware to this day. As they'll tell you, it whips a llama's ass (that sounds like Wesley Willis to us...did you guys *really* make that up?).

2. Make a playlist of what you wish to burn. In Winamp, you do this by clicking the Add button in the Playlist Editor window, selecting Add File(s) (see Figure 4.9), and then picking your MP3s from their directory just as you did with Audio Central in steps 1 and 2 of the preceding section. The tracks shouldn't play immediately, but if they do, stop them.

4.9 Here we are again, creating another playlist. Pretty much the same soft-shoe as earlier.

3. When you first open Winamp, it has a little demo track. To clear it, select Clear Playlist from the Playlist menu in the Playlist Editor window (see Figure 4.10).

   This, as you'll see, is a handy thing to remember. If you're going to be burning MP3s Josh-style, you'll want to clear the playlist every time you set out to make a new CD. You can also save your playlist by clicking Save Playlist under the File menu in the Playlist Editor window.

4.10 Clearing a playlist.

4. Move on over to the Winamp window. There's a little tiny button with the traditional loop-play symbol on it (see Figure 4.11). This button toggles playlist-repeating: when the end of your playlist is reached, it'll start all over again at the top if you have this feature enabled. Disable looping by clicking the button if it's on, or leaving it off if it's off. (You'll know if it's on because there's a little blue indicator light next to the toggle button.)

4.11 You don't want to loop your playlist when you're making WAVs— Winamp will keep going in an endless cycle of decoding. That can be bad.

5. From the Options menu in the Winamp window, choose Preferences, which brings up the Winamp Preferences window (see Figure 4.12). Off to the left, click Output. That changes the right pane into Output Plug-Ins, among which you'll find Nullsoft Disk Writer plug-in. Select that, then click the Configure button at the bottom of the window (see Figure 4.13).

4.12 The Winamp Preferences window, where you'll prepare to make WAVs.

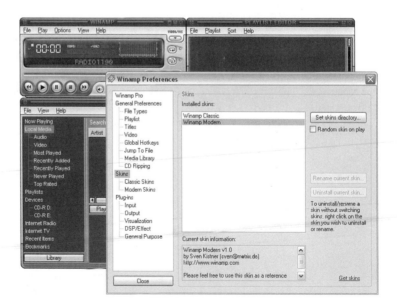

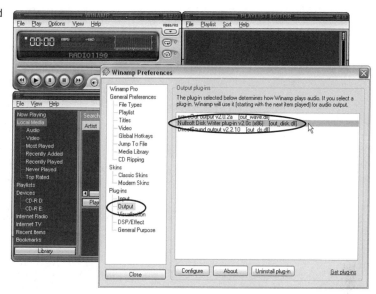

4.13 Here, we've selected Output (left) and Nullsoft Disk Writer plug-in (right), and are going to configure it.

6. In the Disk Writer configuration window that appears, choose a directory—we've chosen our WAV directory here—by clicking that bar (see Figure 4.14). Put a check in the box next to Convert to Format. Directly beneath that, you should see "PCM, 44.100kHz, 16 Bit, Stereo," which, of course is the audio CD standard we've been yakking about. That's the default—if we remember correctly, which we often don't.

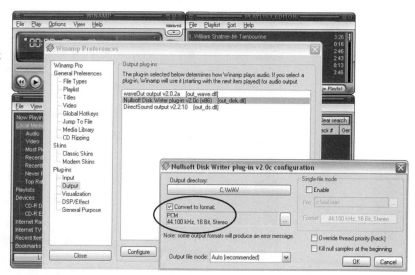

4.14 See the big bar in the Nullsoft Disk Writer configuration window, beneath the words "Output Directory"? Click that bar to select the directory you want your WAVs to land in.

If it doesn't say PCM 44.100kHz..., click the ellipsis next to whatever is there, which brings up a little Sound Selection window (see Figure 4.15). Select PCM for Format, and 44.100 kHz, 16-bit, Stereo for attributes. Click OK to get out of the window.

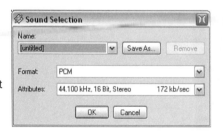

4.15 Clicking on the ellipsis (see Figure 4.14, next to the words "PCM, 44.1...etc.) allows you to precisely configure your output. Here, we want PCM 44.1...you get the idea by now, we're sure.

As far as the Output file mode goes, leave that on Auto. Now click OK, and then click Close to close the Winamp Preferences window.

7. Click the Play button in the Winamp window (see Figure 4.16). Your files will now be decoded to WAV in the directory you chose above. When Winamp's done cooking your MP3s, it might be a good idea to return to the Output Plug-Ins area described in step 5, and select DirectSound Output (see Figure 4.17). Otherwise, you'll be decoding every MP3 you load into a playlist.

4.16 Play initiates the decoding procedure.

4.17 Turn Winamp back into an MP3 player by returning to the Output Plug-Ins area and selecting Direct Sound.

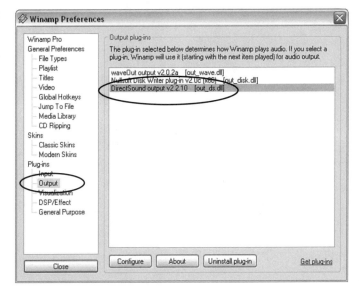

Now you have a bunch of WAV files to work with in your WAV folder. The first thing you'll do is listen to them carefully, making sure each is up to snuff, sonically. If you're happy here, you can queue 'em up and burn 'em with whatever CD-R software you've got handy. Naturally, Josh isn't yet happy with the quality—the WAVs came out great, but they need to be normalized, at the very least. Shoot on over to Chapter 8 to see what makes Josh happy.

The Burn

Nothing special here. Shut off your computer's automated stuff, such as active screensavers or power management features, and quit any open programs. Open your CD recording software, make sure it knows you're burning an audio CD, queue up the tracks, and burn.

Capturing and Recording Digital Streams

Neither of us can get our favorite radio stations on our respective tuners. Bob's favorite, KPIG, is in California, and he's not; Josh's favorite, Radio 1190, is in the next small village over, and despite the fact it's AM, we can't get it in our small village, not when Josh is awake anyhow.

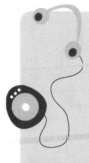

Josh's old roommate used to DJ the midnight-to-6 shift at a Jacuzzi Jazz Radio Station. Josh, too young to buy beer, unemployed, and in need of spiritual guidance, would visit the station often. It was a couple of blocks from the massive bachelor pad inhabited by yet two other guys, one a filmmaker and the other a commercial airline pilot, Josh and his roommate would play chess all night at the station—it's a boring job, being a DJ, despite what one might think.

One night, the DJ looked at Josh in horror, explaining he was experiencing profound gastrointestinal distress in immediate need of attention. Josh, having seen the DJ announce several million times, stepped up to the plate, taking over the mike. This is what he said:

"This is JM taking you into the AM from the PM on the FM dial. You're listening to blah blah blah…." He then spun Kenny G.

The moral of the story is FCC and FAA regulations are sometimes violated by people who drink and play chess, so beware!

Through the miracle of multicasting—that is, in this incarnation, Internet Radio—Bob used to groove to KPIG all day (www.kpig.com), much to Josh's chagrin. (We're at variance often, musicwise—Bob likes olde stuff, like Def Leppard, whereas Josh's tastes are slightly more refined. He loves Jennifer Lopez, for example; she is, after all, just Jenny from the block.) KPIG unfortunately fell victim to certain nameless corporate interests that canned their free stream.

We won't have anything to do with RealAudio—RealPlayer sticks its greasy little tendrils into every nook and cranny of your machine—so Bob won't listen to KPIG anymore. Add to that a $5.95 subscription fee, and, as Donnie Brasco says, "Forget about it." Josh can't say he feels too bad for Bob, especially since Radio 1190's still running an MP3 stream, for free. No RealPlayer, good quality music, good quality stream, for free—life isn't all bad.

There are thousands, maybe millions, of Internet radio stations that don't require the installation of RealPlayer. We urge you to seek these, and listen to them with your favorite MP3 player. In Chapter 4, "Recording MP3s to CD," we highlighted Winamp, a free MP3 player, often recommended by the people who stream audio for your listening pleasure. Have a look at Chapter 4 for further details on Winamp and where to get it. If Winamp isn't to your liking, have a look at the horde of free MP3 players at www.download.com.

TIP

Tuning into an online radio station isn't a big deal at all: usually, it's simply a matter of clicking a link on the station's site. They'll have instructions for you, too, if you encounter a problem.

In this chapter, we're going to skip the steps to tuning in and get straight to it: we're going to show you how to record Internet streams, and burn those to CD. Live recording is a snap, and unattended recording comes in handy if, for instance, you want to catch someone's talk show (though we don't know why you'd want to listen to what's out there—even the self-proclaimed lefties are a smidge to the right of Barry Goldwater) or Shoegazer Hour at a college Internet station but won't be around for it.

NOTE

We're still not quite sure what "Shoegazer" is, but we dig it. Shoegazer Hour usually contains some Julee Cruise, Ride, Curve, Medicine, The Cocteau Twins, that kind of thing.

Attended Capture

We're pretty sure you can locate a free audio streaming recorder someplace, like www.download.com. But for a mere $11.95, you can download the best recorder around: Total Recorder (see Figure 5.1). Simply cruise on over to www.highcriteria.com. Total Recorder is good for not only capturing audio streams, but also for cracking various copy protection schemes placed on certain CDs and DVDs. We'll save instructions on the latter for our upcoming musical, "Steal This Book."

5.1 You can't beat Total Recorder for the price or the functionality.

We're going to configure four things in Total Recorder before we get going here:

○ The folder in which files are saved (we'll once again be using our WAV folder),

○ How often the recording gets split (this so we don't have to deal with a digital audio editor at all),

○ Another item that prevents those silences one occasionally encounters when listening to Internet radio,

and, of course,

○ Our file properties (PCM 44.1kHz, 16-bit, Stereo, but you knew that).

Let's get going:

1. Choose Settings under the Options menu. That brings up the Total Recorder Configuration window (see Figure 5.2). The only two tabs we're going to play with here are the Open/save tab and the Split tab.

5.2 For the moment, we'll be messing around beneath only the Open/save and Split tabs.

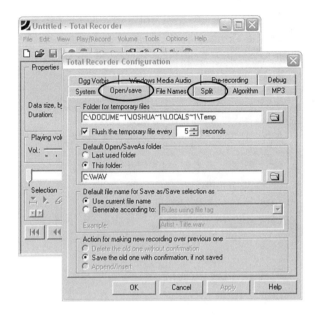

2. Under the Open/save tab, go to the area beneath Default Open/SaveAs folder, and select the radio button next to This Folder (see Figure 5.3). Click the open folder icon, then navigate over to the folder where you wish to store your recording.

5.3 Choose a destination folder for your WAVs.

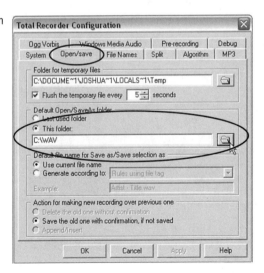

3. Next, click the Split tab and put a check next to Split mode (see Figure 5.4). Click the Conditions button directly next to the Split mode info. The Split Recording Conditions window appears.

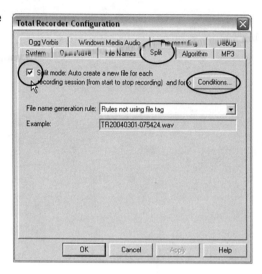

5.4 Selecting Split mode saves us the hassle of going through a digital audio editor to chop up big files.

4. In the Split Recording Conditions window, put a check in the box next to Every X Minutes of Recording (see Figure 5.5). We're going with five minutes, arbitrarily. Click OK.

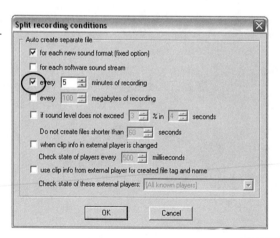

5.5 Five minutes sounds about right for our purposes here.

5. Click Apply when you get back to the Total Recorder Configuration window, and then click OK.

6. Return to the Options menu and choose Recording Source and Parameters. This summons a window called, you guessed it, Recording Source and Parameters (see Figure 5.6). Select the Software radio button; then check the boxes next to Convert Using "Recording Parameters" Specified Below and Remove Silence (Prevent Internet Transmission Gaps).

5.6 Here we're telling Total Recorder to nix the silence during net congestion and to record in accordance with some recording parameters we're about to stipulate.

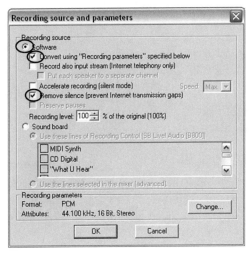

7. Now we're going to need to specify those recording parameters we mentioned in the previous step. If audio CD standard isn't already selected, click the Change button. That brings up a window called Sound Format Selection.

8. In the Sound Format Selection window, choose PCM from the Format drop-down menu, and then choose 44.100 kHz, 16-bit, Stereo from the Attributes drop-down menu (see Figure 5.7). Click OK, and then click OK again when you get back to the Recording Source and Parameters window.

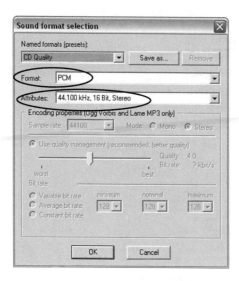

5.7 We're making sure we get WAVs, ready to be burned to CD.

9. Now you should be back in Total Recorder proper. We're now all configured. Leave Total Recorder running.

10. Now get a stream going. We'll get Radio 1190 (www.radio1190.com) going in Winamp by going to their Web site and clicking on their Webcast link (see Figure 5.8). Since we've already got Winamp associated with Internet streams, it'll launch automatically, and begin playing the Webcast.

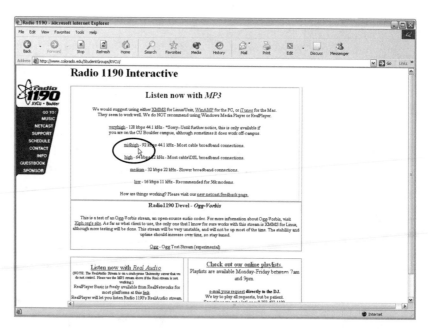

5.8 Clicking on this link launches Radio 1190's netcast.

11. Return, maximize, whatever, to get back to Total Recorder. Click the Big Red Record Button in the lower-right corner (see Figure 5.9). The level meters should start fluctuating, and all kinds of numbers should be appearing in the Properties area (see Figure 5.10). It's recording.

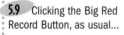

5.9 Clicking the Big Red Record Button, as usual...

5.10 All kinds of activity should begin once you've initiated recording.

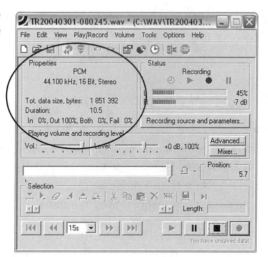

12. Record until you're done. Click the Stop button, directly next to the Big Red Record Button (see Figure 5.11). Now you should have an assortment of WAVs in the directory you specified earlier. We've got three, five-minute WAVs in our WAV folder.

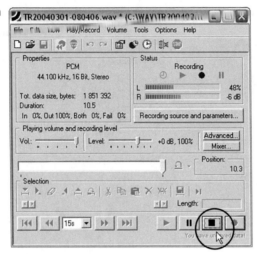

5.11 Click the Stop button when you feel you've recorded enough.

That's it. You can proceed to The Burn now, if you like, or you can watch us program Total Recorder to get something at a later time, when neither of us will be around.

Unattended Capture

If Bob misses Shoegazer Hour, he calls the day a wash and cannot function. We can't have that now, since we're writing a book, so we've set Total Recorder to record Shoegazer Hour. That way, even if Bob isn't around for the live stream, he can listen to the recording of it, and consequently be of good cheer and endless energy. Here's how we did it:

1. Under the Options menu in Total Recorder, choose Schedule. That'll bring up a window called Record/Play Schedule (see Figure 5.12). Click the New button.

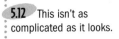
5.12 This isn't as complicated as it looks.

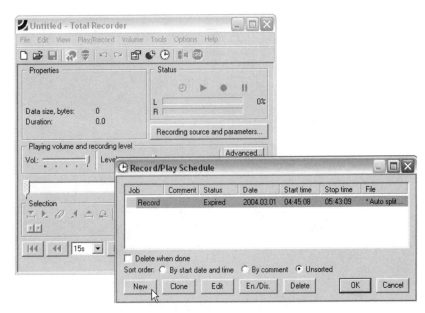

Yeah, that's a little daunting, this Schedule Item window that's appeared. This is a lot easier than it looks, though, since you've already configured Total Recorder. (If you didn't read "Attended Capture" in the previous section, you should do that now.) There isn't really such a thing as Shoegazer Hour, not that we know of, but let's pretend there is.

2. In the Comment field, we're going to type **Shoegazer Hour**. Under Start/Stop time, we're going to choose Daily, and 4:00 AM to 5:00 AM. (It's actually 0400 hours and 0500 hours, Colonel.) Under File Name, we're selecting Auto Create and checking the box next to Split File According to the Specified Conditions. (That's that five-minute condition we put on it earlier, so you don't need to bother with configuring it, if you don't want to). See Figure 5.13 for the whole configuration.

5.13 Here's our whole configuration thus far: date, time, job name, auto split, and all that.

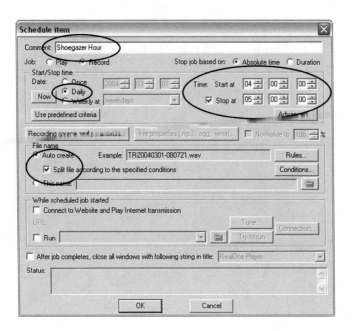

3. Under While Scheduled Job Started, check the box next to Connect to Website and Play Internet Transmission. That brings up a little Web browser called, oddly enough, Total Recorder's Minibrowser. Browse on over to the link that starts your stream—we're browsing over to Radio 1190 for illustrative purposes. Right-click the link to the stream and choose Properties (see Figure 5.14).

5.14 From the Properties window, copy the URL of the link that launches your Webcast.

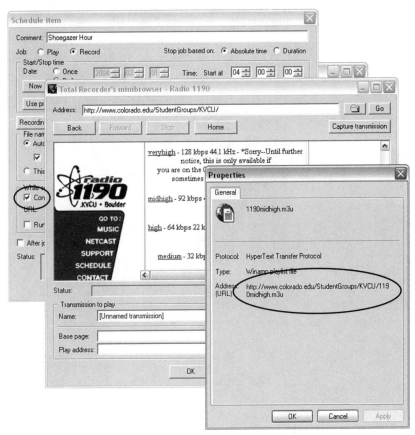

4. Copy the URL from the Properties window—that's where you drag your mouse over a selection, right-click, choose Copy—and then Paste it into Play Address at the bottom of Total Recorder's Minibrowser (see Figure 5.15). Click OK.

5.15 Paste the URL you just copied into the Play Address field.

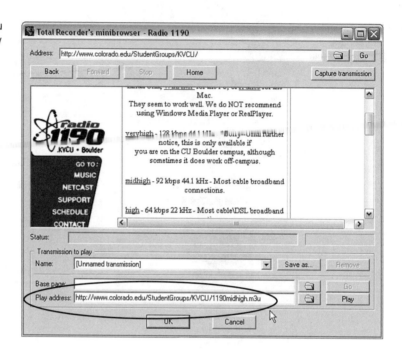

5. Check After Job Completes, Close All Windows with Following String in Title box at the bottom of the Schedule Item window, and select whatever player plays your Webcasts. We're selecting Winamp (see Figure 5.16).

5.16 Choose your player.

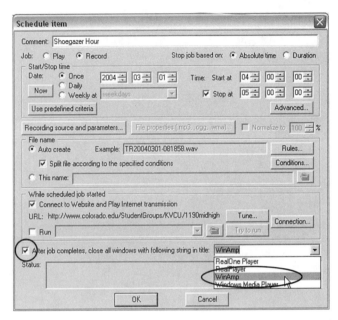

One final thing...

6. Leave Total Recorder running someplace, minimized if you want, and turn off all your power management features (standby, hibernate, shut off hard disks, and so on), except for the monitor.

Now, every day at 4 AM, Total Recorder will record Shoegazer Hour. When we get to our desks in the morning, we'll have 12, five-minute tracks ready to be burned to CD.

Pretty cool, huh?

The Burn

If you decided to chop your file up into more manageable pieces, make sure you queue them up in order in your Audio CD layout. You'll also want to burn Disc-At-Once, making sure there's no gap between your tracks. Otherwise, it's a plain-old standard audio burn.

Restoring and Recording Cassette Tapes

Up until now, you probably haven't required any special equipment to copy and burn your own CDs—besides, of course, your computer, your CD-recordable drive and software, some kind of sound card or built-in sound output device, speakers, maybe some headphones, WAVs, and whatnot.

Now we're going back in time a little bit. Back in the late '70s through the late '80s, our music collections consisted of records and tapes, which we'll be digitizing, cleaning up, and burning to CD in the ensuing paragraphs. (Have no fear; it's much easier than you might think.)

There are a number of reasons, at least on our end, for getting our tapes onto CD. Mostly, for us, it's all about nostalgia and sentiment. Remember getting mix tapes from your high school sweetheart? We don't: nobody liked Josh in high school and Bob was already using Grecian Formula and reading *AARP* magazine by the time CD rolled around. We did, however, listen to a lot of wonderful and sometimes rare music on cassette tape, Bob during his bouts with gastro-intestinal distress from having forgotten to eat/drink his morning fiber, and Josh during his moments of abject loneliness and existential alienation. Man, those were days.

Nowadays, cassettes get a bad rap. But cassettes don't have to languish in the bottom of a drawer forever—your old compilation tape from 1986 can be restored to its former glory.

Fortunately, connecting your tape deck (also referred to as a *cassette* deck) to your computer isn't at all difficult. You'll need a cable to connect the two devices, (more on that later in this chapter) and you'll definitely want to use a digital audio editor to clean up what gets recorded (unless you'd enjoy, for nostalgia's sake, listening to a disc that sounds like a cassette tape).

You'll also need to take a couple of necessary precautions to prevent any further noise—electrical noise, specifically—from being added to your recording, but those, too, won't break anybody's back.

If you don't have a tape deck, not to worry. Even the expensive ones are cheap these days. You should be able to find a used tape deck with a single tray at a thrift store for under $20. New is best, of course, but used will certainly do, just so long as the heads are still mostly intact.

As with many things, it's hard to tell just by looking what kind of shape the innards are in—Josh, for example, is extraordinarily handsome on the outside, but has lungs fulla tar, a caterwauling liver, and a broken heart, damn her—so don't buy a tape deck from the pawn shop unless they let you have a listen first. Keep in mind, too, you're only going to need one tray, so that'll knock a bunch of money off your purchase. (If all you've got is a boom box, that'll work too, so long as there's a line-out jack on the back—more on that in just a bit.)

NOTE If you do have a tape deck, or procure one, it's probably been shelved for awhile, and the heads and capstans haven't seen a cleaning since the Iran-Contra scandal. Since our aim is to get the best signal onto our machines so we don't have to spend a lot of time restoring, it's a good idea to clean your tape heads first. It's a pretty easy procedure: dampen—dampen, not soak—a tightly wound Q-Tip in isopropyl alcohol, and gently wipe down the places where tape of days gone by has passed—the heads, the capstans, the idler tire, and so on—until no more gunk appears on your Q-Tips (see Figure 6.1). Try very hard not to lose any cotton in there. (Just as with your eardrums, wielding the Q-Tip clumsily in the tape deck may lead to a lifetime of silence—but without the loud pop preceding.)

6.1 These are the innards of a cassette deck. Clean your tape heads of the detritus of days gone by with a *tightly wound* Q-Tip *dampened* with isopropyl alcohol.

Tape heads

NOTE Some people swear by demagnetizers, too, but neither of us, having used them, has noticed any appreciable difference. But, as always, we defer to your ears, so give it a whirl if you feel like it.

Unplug Before You Plug In

Before you get started, we're going to have you power down here, turning your computer and other devices off (especially powered speakers, if you have those, this to avert potentially blowing them out). Once that's done, unplug all extraneous devices, including any printers, scanners, Zip drives, modems, and the like, leaving only your computer, monitor, and powered speakers plugged into one power strip. If you have multiple power strips, pick one, and unplug the other, discarding it for the moment. That done, go ahead and plug in your cassette deck.

At this point, you should have only four things plugged in—at most—and all those things should be plugged into one strip, or at the very least, the same wall outlet:

○ Computer

○ Monitor

○ Powered speakers

○ Cassette deck

Why have only the one power strip with minimal connections? We're trying to avoid adding the insidious 60-cycle hum and buzz to our recording. Since everyone knows at least one guitarist, everyone's heard buzz: that's that jarring "gazzat" noise that occurs when a guitar is plugged into a live amp. Some amps, good ones even, hum all the time. That hum is the sound of the electricity being used to power the device, and the sound of electricity in general, if you were able to hear it all the time. However charming that sound may be when your friend is desperately trying to get his fingers on the proper frets for "Iron Man," it's not fun to have that sound on your recordings.

NOTE

Sometimes it's the case that 60-cycle hum is introduced not by your equipment, but rather the mastering studio's equipment—it's part of the actual recording. A bit of good news here: hum is located at a very specific frequency—60Hz in America, 50Hz across the pond, just by the nature of the way we're wired for electricity—and it's a well-known phenomenon, so there's a filter designed specifically for it in most digital audio editors, called a *notch filter*. We'll go into detail about that filter in the next chapter, "Recording and Restoring Vinyl."

For now, odds are good that if you're plugged in the way we showed you, you won't need to notch anything out. That's the cool way of saying that, by the way, so now you can run around being cool at audio engineer cocktail parties. For example, say something like, "So dude was doin' his check-sibilants soft-shoe and dude kept hearin' 60-cycle from the monitor, so we looked for the ground loop, couldn't find one, so we just notched it 'cuz the band was too stoned to even know." You'll be a hit, guaranteed.

Plug In

Now, while you're still completely powered down, we're going to run a cable from your tape deck to your computer. What kind of cable you'll use will depend on what kind of inputs you have available to you (that is, what kind of holes you have on your sound card or built into your machine), and what kind of output scheme you've decided on. You have several options for connecting your tape deck and your computer:

○ **Mini-jack or Y-cable to your line-in:** This type of connection, which works on either a PC or Macintosh, requires either a Y cable or an RCA cable with a stereo-mini adapter attached (see Figure 6.2). These days, Y cables often ship with software and drivers, so you may already have one of these (if not, Radio Shack will sell you one cheap). One end of the cable terminates in the right and left RCA channels—the red and white connections you've likely seen before when hooking up stereo equipment—and the other end terminates in a stereo-mini plug, the same thing you see on headphones, your computer's external speakers, that kind of thing.

Plug the RCA end of the cable into the right and left channels of the line-out on the back of your cassette deck, and plug the stereo-mini end into the line-in on your sound card or mainboard, which most often is demarcated by four parentheses shot through with an arrow: — ((>)). It also might simply say "line in." Now you're connected. Stay powered down though, for the moment. (For a crude representation, see Figures 6.3 and 6.4.)

6.2 This is a Y cable, commonly shipped these days with CD-R software and CD-R drive bundles.

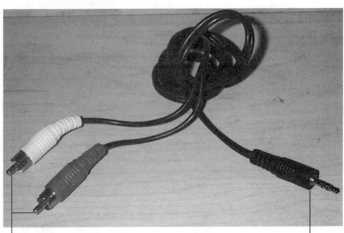

The RCA plugs plug into the line-out on your cassette deck.

The stereo-mini end runs to your line-in, whether that's a line-in in your sound card or a mic jack on your Mac.

6.3 Up at the very top of this PC sound card, you can see the line-in jack. Notice the arrow points inward, not outward. Your speakers should be plugged into the outward jack just below it.

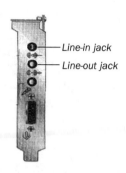

Line-in jack
Line-out jack

6.4 On a Mac, the line-in and mic jack are one and the same. (On this iMac, it's the plug in the top-left corner.)

The line-in/mic jack

○ **RCA cable to sound card's RCA jacks** (see Figure 6.5)**:** Connecting with an RCA cable is pretty much the same procedure as connecting with a Y cable or mini-jack line-in. Connect your RCA cable—if you don't have any RCA cable, it's available at just about any electronics store, from Best Buy to Soundtrack—from the line-out on your tape deck to the RCA plug on your sound card. If your sound card comes with an RCA-in port, you're better off choosing this connection option, not just because it'll render a better recording, but also because you have many options as far as cable goes, from the cheapo RCA that came with your receiver (or another peripheral) to pricey, gold-tipped Monster Cable (www.monstercable.com). Again, stay powered down.

TIP

High-quality cable can make a big difference, just because it's not so suscepti-ble to stray electromagnetic radiation from, say, a monitor, CPU, or nearby transformer. That's what that whole "super-shielded!" thing featured on the package in a little yellow explosion means.

6.5 Many of the better (and occasionally more expensive) sound cards feature RCA-in, and you have a wide choice of RCA cables, from the standard-issue, cheapo (featured here) to Monster Cable.

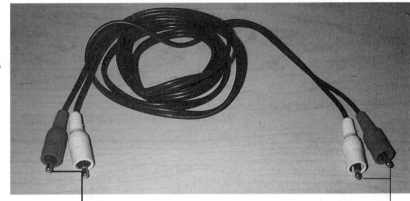

One end of the plug plugs into the line-out on your cassette deck.

The other end plugs into your sound card.

○ **RCA cable to a USB audio capture device:** If you happened to pick up a USB audio capture device, they typically feature RCA connections. Simply run an RCA-to-RCA connection, as described in the preceding bullet item after you plug your device into your USB port or hub. (Please pay a visit to Chapter 2, "Hardware and Software," for more detail on USB audio capture devices.)

There's one final thing to do before we power up. Because tapes and decks function by way of magnetism, it's best to keep your deck away from possible sources of wayward electromagnetic radiation, if you can. Monitors, especially old CRT things, emit all kinds of stray radiation, as does your CPU, to a lesser degree. Once again, the reason to do this is we're trying to get as clean a signal as possible going in so that we don't have to deal with a noisy recording when editing time comes around.

Power Up

Now that you're done plugging in, power up. If you can control the volume of your powered speakers with a knob or some such, turn them down pretty far. We'll bring those back on up in a minute. Something to note: once we get recording underway, you can blast them or turn them off as you choose—the sound issuing from your speakers isn't the signal being recorded. Strange, but true.

Preparing for Recording on Windows

Now we're going to get into your computer's audio controls in order to prepare your computer for the signal—that is, your tunes—that'll be issuing from your tape deck in a minute. On a Windows machine, you should see a little loudspeaker next to the proper time of day in your taskbar. (If you've got too much happening on your PC, you may have to click the left-pointing arrow adjacent to the clock to "Show Hidden Icons"; the speaker will appear first or second on the right.)

1. Double-click the speaker icon on your Windows taskbar to bring up the Play Control window (see Figure 6.6) which resembles a mixing board with slider bars and balance controls. But we're only going to be messing with one feature here, specifically, the line-in control.

6.6 In Windows, access the Play Control window by double-clicking the loudspeaker icon in your taskbar. Look for the Line-In control.

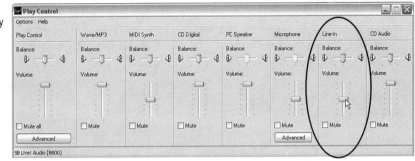

If you don't see the Line-In control in this window, choose Properties from the Options pull-down menu. The Properties window appears. In this window, you'll see a drop-down menu called Mixer Device, a set of radio buttons (select Playback, if it isn't already selected), and a scrolling list of check boxes called Show the Following Volume Controls. Scroll down through the list until you come across Line-In (see Figure 6.7). Check the box next to that, and click OK to close the window. You should now see Line-In listed among the controls in the Play Control window.

NOTE The Mixer Device is going to be, or should be, your sound card or audio capture device. If it's not, select it from the drop-down menu. Note that it will vary from PC to PC, and not necessarily be the same brand indicated in Figure 6.7.

6.7 Select Line-In by checking the box next to it (if it's not already checked).

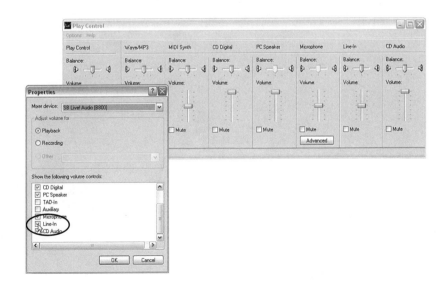

2. If the "Mute" check box below the Line-In control has a check in it, remove it by clicking the box. Next, pull the Line-in slider bar all the way down, push the Play Control slider bar all the way up (see Figure 6.8).

6.8 We've moved the Play Control slider all the way up, and the Line In slider all the way down.

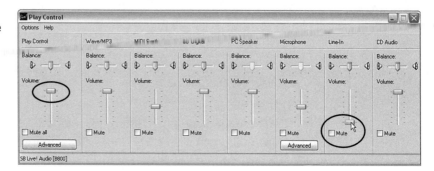

3. Put a tape in your tape deck, and begin playing the tape. Not to insult anyone's intelligence, but you do this by pressing the Play button beneath the deck's tray.

4. When you're pretty sure there's music playing, slowly move the slider bar under Line-In in the Play Control window upward (see Figure 6.9). You should start hearing your tape playing over your speakers at a gradually increased volume.

6.9 Slide the Line-In bar upwards until you've got a comfortable listening volume.

5. Now, fiddle away until you're happy with what you're hearing. You can mess around with the slider bar beneath Line In and turn the knob on your speakers all you like. You can also mess around with the Play Control slider bar, but keep in mind that the Play Control slider bar is the master volume control for everything (MP3s, WAVs, CDs, and DVDs) so that's one to keep on the high side. You can adjust the various other slider bars to your taste for other functions, such as CD and MP3 play-back. You can also expect to have some control of your input volume from within your recording software of choice.

TIP

We tend to keep the Play Control slider bar all the way up, all the time, just because it's practical.

Preparing for Recording

Naturally, things are a little easier on a Mac. Still, we'll walk you through set-up step by step, just as we did for Windows users.

NOTE

PC Users: You can skip steps 1-5 here and instead pick up with step 1 at the bottom of page 119.

1. From the Apple menu in the top-left corner of your screen, choose System Preferences.

2. In the System Preferences window that appears, click the Sound icon to bring up the Sound window. Click the Input tab, then select your sound device from the window that appears (see Figure 6.10). Here, we've set up to go into the Built-In sound port, so we've selected Built-In in the window. Below, in the Settings for Selected Device slider, set your input volume and your output volume (which you can mute if you don't want to hear what's coming through the tape deck). You can also select the Show Volume in Menu Bar check box—this lets you adjust the volume on the fly by selecting the speaker icon in the upper-right corner of your screen.

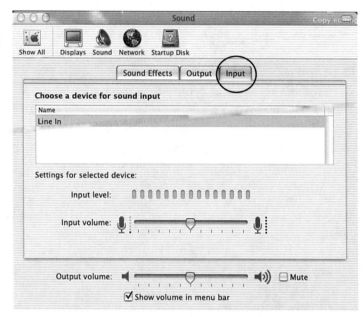

6.10 On a Mac, select your sound device from the dialog. We've selected the Built In port.

3. Still in the Sound window, click the Output tab and move the Output volume slider left.

4. Now play your cassette, and gradually move the Output Volume slider right. You should now be able to hear your cassette playing over your speakers. As we suggested to the PC people in step 5 of the preceding section, fiddle until you're happy.

Dolby Noise Reduction

Back in the day, Ray Dolby devised a means by which to reduce the high-frequency noise (appropriately called "tape-hiss") that's a natural part of any analog cassette tape. This hiss is a function of the magnetic principles at work during cassette tape playback, and it's concentrated at the high end of the frequency spectrum, that is, the "treble" end—think Darth Vader's "pah," as opposed to his "poh," or Trio's "pah" as opposed to "poh" in "Boom Boom."

The idea behind Dolby Noise Reduction (NR) is that if you enhance the high-frequency audio signal—the actual high notes and whatnot of a voice, piano, trumpet, and so on—you'll drown out the hiss. This is an example of "signal masking," essentially, as we talked about in Chapter 4, "Recording MP3s to CD." Then, on the playback deck, you'd push a little Dolby NR button, which would bring the high frequencies back down, along with the already drowned-out hiss.

If you happen to have some or all flavors of Dolby NR on your deck, try them out, see what you think. Off, you'll have a crisp, hissy signal; on, you'll get a flatter signal, mainly devoid of hiss. Either way, you'll be rid of the hiss altogether once we process what we record in our digital audio editor.

What you hear coming out of your speakers is probably pleasing to your ear, but what your computer hears is a different story altogether. You're hearing volume, while your computer is hearing *amplitude* (see Chapter 8, "Polishing Your Compilation Disc," for a full definition of "amplitude"), which, in this instance, is the electrical "strength" of the incoming signal. You're going to have to adjust your machine's ears to mimic your own to avoid sonic overload.

5. If your tape is still playing, go ahead and stop it. You don't have to rewind just yet, but you can if you want.

There aren't any OS controls on a Mac for this, so you Mac folks don't need to mess around so much here. PC people, however, have another thing to do. (Do continue to pay attention though, Mac people, because we're about to record our cassette to hard disk, illustrating the procedure on a PC. For all intents and purposes, it's the same thing: we're just picking an arbitrary digital audio editor and OS.)

1. Once again, on your PC, double-click the loudspeaker icon, bringing up the Play Control window. From the Options menu, choose Properties to make the Properties window appear. This time, click the Recording radio button (see Figure 6.11). Just as in the Playback window, you'll see your selected audio device—which should be the sound card you plugged into (if not, select it from the drop-down menu)—and at the bottom of the window, a list of volume controls. If the box next to Line-In isn't checked, check it. Click OK to exit the window.

6.11 Now we're in Windows' Recording Control. Be sure there's a check beside Line-In so that it appears among your recording devices.

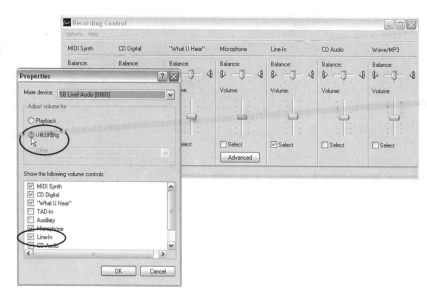

2. Now you should have a window called Recording Control that looks almost exactly like the Playback Control window. Bring the slider beneath Line-In all the way down, and put a check in the Select box beneath it, if it's not there already (see Figure 6.12).

What you're doing here is putting foam earplugs in your computer; it won't pick up what you heard at all so long as that slider is all the way down. Leave this window open, minimizing it if you wish.

6.12 Bring the Line-In slider down so you can adjust your recording levels later. Notice, too, we've checked the Select check box beneath Line-In.

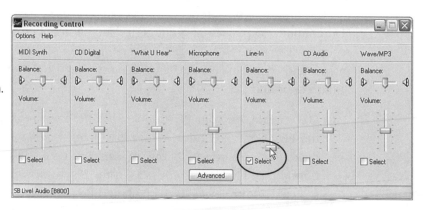

3. Fire up your digital audio editing software. For this example, we're using Adobe's Audition 1 for Windows (www.adobe.com). Adobe recently acquired Syntrillium's Cool Edit Pro 2.1—long a staple of audio recording, restoring, altering, and editing—and renamed it Audition 1.0. Very little has changed, but we're estimating that Audition will be receiving an overhaul sometime in 2004. Our guess is that little will be added or subtracted from the current iteration of Audition, except maybe some cosmetic changes to the user interface.

NOTE

If you happened to miss our discussion of digital audio editors in Chapter 2, we'll refer you there now so that you can have a general look at what these things do. Chapter 2 also includes some recommendations of packages you may wish to try and/or purchase—from the free to the inexpensive to the exorbitant. Most digital audio editors work pretty much the same way, so it's easy to extrapolate: they all sort of look the same and do the same things, whether you're using a package for the Mac or for the PC.

Mac people have a lovely array of digital audio editors to choose from, and they very closely resemble their PC counterparts (and are naturally easier to work with). Though we'll be working with a digital audio editor built for and run on the PC, you'll immediately notice the similarities between what you've got running on your Mac and the software we're using.

4. In Audition, the first thing you'll want to do is make sure it knows where the audio signal is coming from. You do this by first choosing Device Properties from the Options menu (see Figure 6.13). This brings up a tabbed window called Device Properties. Click the Wave Out tab first, and select the sound device you've got your speakers plugged into from the drop-down menu in the upper-left corner (see Figure 6.14).

You're doing this to ensure Audition plays what you're about to record through your speakers—you can't edit what you can't hear, right? Check the box next to Use This Device in Edit View, too, if it's not already checked.

You don't need to do anything else here, but, if you're interested in what's going on, check out the Help file. Yawner, we think, but different strokes, you know...

6.13 In Adobe Audition, choose Device Properties from the Options menu.

6.14 Here, under the Wave Out tab, we're picking our Output Device. (It's a fancy way of saying "your computer speakers.")

5. Next, click the Wave In tab, choose whatever audio device you plugged your deck into from the drop-down menu in the upper-left corner, and then check the box next to Use This Device in Edit View, just as you did under the Wave Out tab (see Figure 6.15). This is to direct Audition's attention to that port, recording whatever should happen across it. Now, click OK to exit the window (unless, of course, you're interested in all the other things going on beneath this tab—again, the Help file is where it's at).

6.15 Now we're choosing our input device—in this case, the sound card into which we plugged our line from the deck.

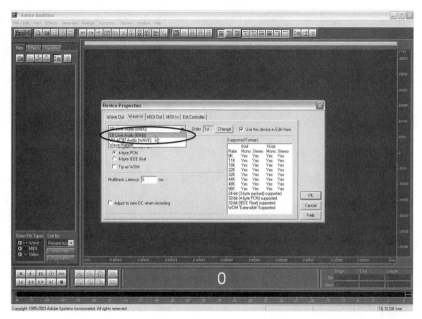

6. Audition may default to what's called Multitrack view. If you're seeing a lot of bars stacked vertically called Track 1, Track 2, and so on, you're in Multitrack view (see Figure 6.16). You don't want to be here. Get out by pressing F12, or by clicking the leftmost button in the toolbar, below the drop-down menus. Now you're in Edit view.

6.16 This is what the Multitrack view looks like in Audition. If you find yourself here, leave.

There are a couple other settings Audition defaults to that you might not want. The first is the live update feature, which, if left on, draws your waveform up on-the-fly, sucking up precious processing resources. To turn it off, click Options and then choose Settings. In the Settings window, under the General tab, remove the check next to Live Update During Recording (see Figure 6.17). Close the Settings window.

6.17 Remove the check from the Live Update During Recording option— it sucks up unnecessary processor cycles.

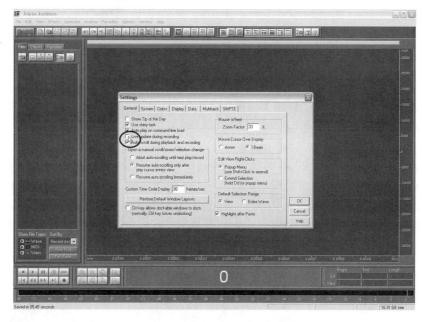

The second thing is the way time is displayed. Right-click the big "0" down toward the bottom of Audition (see Figure 6.18). From the pop-up menu that appears, choose which type of time display you want. (We usually go with Decimal.)

6.18 Choose whichever time display you like.

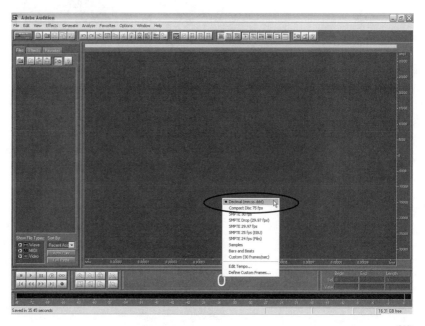

7. Choose New from the File menu. This summons a window called New Waveform. In this window, under Sample Rate, select 44100; under Channels, select the radio box next to Stereo; and under Resolution, select 16-bit (see Figure 6.19). You've just set the parameters—in case you hadn't guessed—for recording a waveform that comports with the CD-Audio standard. (You can read all about that, if you haven't already, in Chapter 1, "Diving Right In.") Click OK.

6.19 We're all set to record a standard Audio CD track to hard disk—having selected a 44100 (Hz) sample rate and a 16-bit resolution, all in stereo—so that we may manipulate it, clean it up, then burn it.

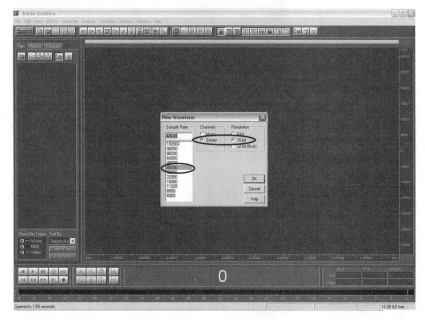

8. Play your tape again until you hear something, and then click the little red Record button in the lower-left corner of Audition (see Figure 6.20). Bring up your Recording Control window we had you leave open a little while back, so that it's superimposed over Audition, toward the high side. Slowly bring the Line-In slider upward, until two pulsing lines appear at the bottom of the Audition screen (see Figure 6.21). Those pulsing lines are your record levels.

6.20 When you're all set, click the Record button.

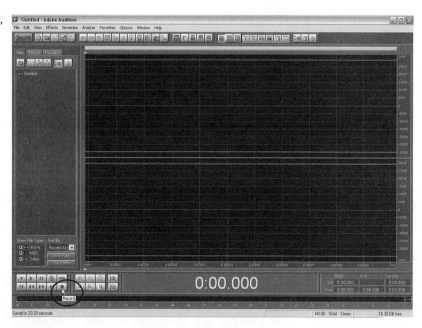

6.21 Raise the Line-In in Windows' Recording Control until you've got good recording levels.

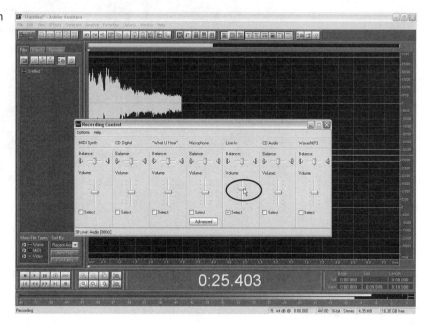

9. Now begins the delicate dance of getting your record levels high enough to have a good signal to work with, but not so high that you get distortion in your recording. If your levels are too high, you'll get a searing case of what's known as "clipping" (see Figure 6.22), which will be indicated to you by the little boxes off to the right of the pulsing lines. (They'll be filled solid red, and they'll stay that way.)

If, on the other hand, your record levels are too low, you'll have to process them digitally—it's a procedure called gain normalization, which we'll show you in just a second—which is fine, but keep in mind, the more you digitally mess with what you record, the more likely you are to lose fidelity.

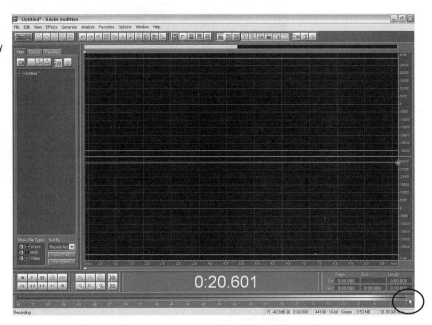

6.22 Ack, clipping. The arrow is pointing at the boxes that will fill and stay filled to alert you to the fact you've clipped.

TIP

That's a rule to live by, by the way: try to do as little as possible to what you record, digitally speaking, so as to keep fidelity to the original signal. This is why we insisted earlier that you get as good a signal as possible going in: moving your deck around, plugging into the same power strip, that kind of thing.

10. When you're happy with your levels, stop recording—do this by clicking the square Stop button up and to the left of the Record button (see Figure 6.23)—and stop and rewind your tape. From the File menu, choose Close, and don't Save Changes when that dialog box comes up. You can minimize, or even close, the Record Control window now.

6.23 The arrow here points to the Stop button. Click it once you're content with your recording levels.

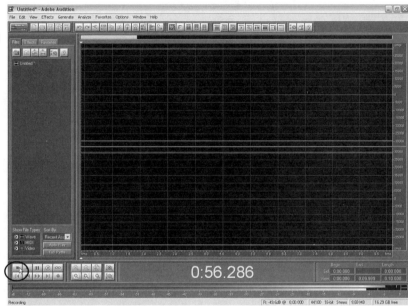

If you happen across clipping during recording, you're going to have to start all over again, bringing the Line-In slider bar down before you begin. You can't bring your Line-In signal down during recording, because doing so will leave you with wild variance in amplitude, and consequently, wild variance in volume during playback—very unpleasant.

1. Again, choose New from the File menu, and again do what you did just a second ago in steps 12-15: 44100 sampling rate, stereo, 16-bit, OK. This time, start recording in Audition before you begin playing your tape.

You're doing this because you'll have a big sample of hiss to work with right up front when it comes time to remove the hiss from your recording. The "silence" between songs also works. It's not really silent there—but a bigger sample of hiss is better, simply because Audition will have a better idea of the kinds of noise present on your tape (and a better idea of what to remove) the longer it gets to see it, the same way that studying a Picasso for an hour leads to a better comprehension than if you were rushed past it by a tour guide who probably has a memorized script from which he darest not stray.

2. When the tape stops, stop recording, just as you did before. Now Audition will draw up your waveform for you (see Figure 6.24). Save your waveform by choosing Save As from the File menu, giving it a name (and if you wish, a whole folder devoted to it—that's what we do, to keep track of these things), and saving it as a Windows PCM file. (Select that, if it's not already selected from the scroll menu at the bottom of the window.) Click Save, and close that file (File > Close).

3. Now flip your tape, and record the other side, saving that as "Side2" or whatever you like, in whatever folder you like. We're recording Bruce Springsteen's *Nebraska*—appropriate enough for this chapter, since it was mastered from a home-recorded cassette he carried around in his back pocket for six months, trying to figure out what to do with it—so we've named our files Nebraska1 and Nebraska2.

6.24 Our cassette side, digitally represented in a waveform.

NOTE

Didja know Bruce Springsteen's mother's maiden name is Zirilli? And that Bruce Willis stuttered as a boy? And that Bruce Jenner won a gold medal at the 1976 Olympics? And that Bruce Hornsby doesn't play tennis? And that Lenny Bruce got in trouble for his comic act? And that Robert the Bruce wasn't actually alive during William Wallace's lifetime? And that *Tron* star Bruce Boxleitner is the brother-in-law of Sara Gilbert of *Roseanne* fame? And that Josh once received a nice bruce on his eye from a bouncer at a bar? All somewhat true, guaranteed.

Recording is now complete. You now have two very large files somewhere—we hope you know where (ours are in a folder devoted specifically to WAVs, the one we mentioned earlier)—on your hard disk.

Taking a Noiseprint and Dehissing

Now we're going to begin restoring our recording. Open Audition (if it is not already) and then open one of the files you recorded in the preceding section—we're going with Nebraska1.wav here—by choosing Open from the File menu. And rats, it looks like we didn't get as much hiss as we would've liked at the beginning of the recording (see Figure 6.25). That's OK, we'll take our hiss sample somewhere else: the space between track four and track five looks good. Incidentally, the large blocks of the waveform are songs, and the little spaces between them are, in theory, "silence," but they're not exactly silent—they're hissy, so we're heading on in there.

6.25 Darn, say we, not enough silence at the beginning of our waveform (highlighted). Fortunately, you can grab hiss from anywhere.

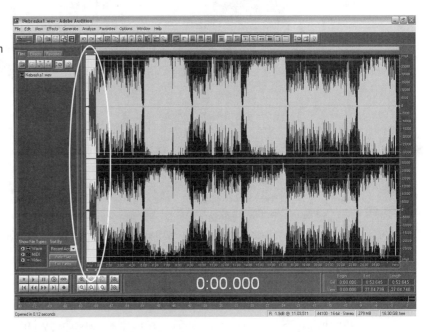

TIP

Sometimes you'll want to take a sample from the beginning of your recording no matter what, because your sound capture device might introduce a little of its own noise. It's good to be rid of that, too, because it probably persists through your whole recording.

1. We're selecting the area of "silence" approximately by clicking and hold-ing on the waveform toward the end of song four 4, and dragging into the very early part of song 5, releasing the mouse button there (see Figure 6.26). Now we're going to zoom in on that area so we can select a more precise area between those two songs.

6.26 We've highlighted an alternative hiss area.

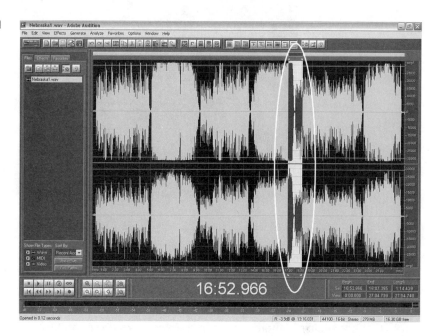

2. You zoom in by clicking the Zoom to Selection button, directly to the right of the Record button we used just a second ago (see Figure 6.27). Clicking this button, you might have guessed, takes you to your selection on your waveform.

6.27 Zooming in, we find a nice chunk of silence. (Visually, it's the flat area between strong signals.)

16:52.966

TIP

Because speaker static sounds a lot like hiss (it is hiss, actually, scientifically speaking, the orchestra of magnetism) and to block out the ambient noise of a room (traffic, wind, chatting monks, etc.), we like to put on headphones here. Most desktop speakers these days have a headphone jack on them, so we generally plug in there, and turn the speakers down until we hear no more static.

3. Now we make another selection, just as we did in step 1, by clicking and dragging, over that mostly flat line (see Figure 6.28). That's hiss there, and that's what we want Audition to get an idea of. Don't select anything other than that flat line; otherwise Audition, when you run the DeHiss filter, will mistake music for noise, and you don't want that— Audition will pull chunks of song all along the waveform. It sounds funky and arty, but that's not our aim here, right? We're just trying to capture a clean recording.

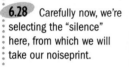

6.28 Carefully now, we're selecting the "silence" here, from which we will take our noiseprint.

4. From the Effects menu, choose Noise Reduction, and choose Hiss Reduction from the submenu. In the Hiss Reduction window that pops up, click the Get Noise Floor button beneath the grid (see Figure 6.29). That grid represents frequency (the x-axis) versus amplitude (the y-axis).

You'll notice we're down at a low amplitude (the hiss signal is never that strong), and we're all the way across the frequency spectrum. What gets drawn in that grid after you click the Get Noise Floor button is the threshold beneath which everything, sonically, will get cut entirely. You can cut this stuff altogether simply because it is at this low amplitude; the higher amplitude stuff will drown it out anyway, except at the very high frequencies where hiss is concentrated (and where our ears are more sensitive).

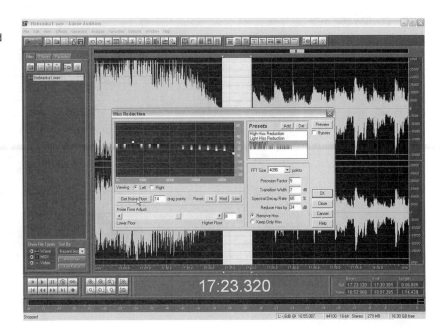

6.29 Click Get Noise Floor when you've found your "silence," and have opened the Hiss Reduction window.

NOTE Once again, there are a bunch of other settings in here that you can learn all about in the Help file. The defaults are good, but of course, feel free to fiddle.

5. Still in Hiss Reduction, click the Preview button in the upper-right corner of the window. If you don't hear anything, good! Click the Preview button, which has miraculously transformed into a button called Stop (see Figure 6.30). Now click the radio button next to Keep Only Hiss, down toward the bottom of the window. Click Preview again. If you hear hiss, good! Click the Stop button. You've probably got an accurate sample here of what noise is to be removed from your recording.

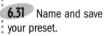

6.30 Mess around a bunch in here, listening to your hiss, then the silence, then hiss, then silence, until you're happy.

6. In the Presets area to the right of the grid, click the Add button. A window appears, asking you to name this preset (see Figure 6.31). We've named ours Nebraska1. Click OK. Now Nebraska1 will appear among the list of presets.

6.31 Name and save your preset.

7. Don't exit the Hiss Reduction window by way of the OK button. Rather, click Cancel. Don't worry, your preset will be saved.

8. Zoom all the way out to your whole waveform by clicking the Zoom Out Full Both Axis button, located at the upper-right corner of the zoom buttons, where you clicked Zoom In To Selection (see Figure 6.32). From the Edit menu, choose Select Entire Wave. Your whole waveform will be highlighted, blue on white, rather than green on black.

6.32 Zoom out all the way by clicking Zoom Out Full Axis (the button beneath the arrow), then choose Select Entire Wave from the Edit menu.

9. Open the Hiss Reduction window again, click the Preview button, and shift alternately between the Keep Only Hiss and Remove Hiss radio buttons as often as you like, the former to hear what's being removed, and the latter to ensure your recording sounds good with this filter applied. Listen, previewing, for a long time.

If it happens that you're hearing music during the Keep Only Hiss, and your tunes sound that great during Remove Hiss, you're going to need to find another area of hiss—either between songs or at the beginning or end of your waveform—and repeat the Get Noise Floor procedure we just described. It happens. No worries.

10. Click Cancel again to depart the Hiss Reduction window.

11. When you're happy with your Preset—we're happy with ours—select your entire waveform, if it isn't already (From the Edit menu, choose Select Entire Wave, as we did earlier). Open the Hiss Reduction window, select the preset you just created, and select the radio button next to Remove Hiss. This time, click OK to close the window (see Figure 6.33).

That runs the filter over your entire waveform, removing all the hiss. A dialog box appears, indicating the filter's progress and the ETA for completion. This takes several minutes, so you can go spend time with the kids now, or do whatever you feel like doing.

6.33 This time, click OK in the Hiss Reduction window. This will remove all hiss from the waveform.

You'll need to return at some point to repeat the whole of this procedure with side two of your tape. Now that you know how to do it, though, it's easy enough, right?

Track Splitting and Cleanup

Generally speaking, we recommend against using automatic track splitters. Many works include silence as part of a whole—from John Cage's body of composition to the Contours' "Do You Love Me?" with its epochal fake ending—and we don't want to end up with two tracks (or 100, in the instance of John Cage) that are supposed to be one track. And as we said, what we hear as silence is not always silence—particularly on a scratchy record—so a track splitter might even miss a track break now and again. And it's just as easy to manually split your waveform. The human being, in this instance, will be more precise than the machine.

NOTE There are several ways to do this, but we've found this one best, because not only can you select your tunes with precision, but you can also trim the silence on either end of what will become your track to be burned to CD.

1. Select the first song and some of the next generally by clicking it, holding the mouse button down and dragging. Zoom into your selection by clicking the Zoom to Selection button, as you did when you began taking your noiseprint. Now, as precisely as possible, click and drag from the beginning to the end of that first song, trying to get just the song, and not the silence before or after (see Figure 6.34). Right-click your selection, and choose Add to Cue list from the menu that appears, or simply press F8. Zoom back on out by clicking the Zoom Out Full Both Axis button.

6.34 Highlight a song, right-click it, and add it to the Cue List.

2. Repeat step 1 with each song, selecting a little of the song before and a little of the song after, then zooming in, and then choosing Add to Cue List or pressing the F8 button. The silence between songs is more evident that way.

3. That done, open the Cue List by selecting it from the View menu up top (see Figure 6.35). In the Cue List window, you should see all the cues you placed. We have six in this instance. Hold down the Ctrl key on your keyboard, and click each cue, in order. This selects all of your tracks.

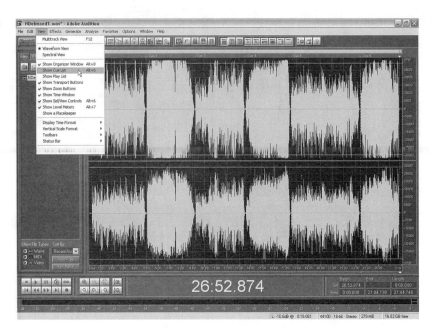

6.35 Choose Show Cue List from the View menu.

4. If the Edit Cue Info isn't already visible, click the button in the lower-left corner called Edit Cue Info (see Figure 6.36). You should see, off to the right, a scroll menu called Type. Drop that down and select Track. That should change the Type in your cue list from all Basic to all Track.

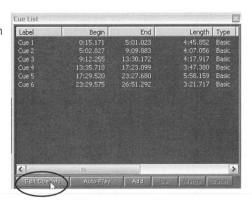

6.36 Click Edit Cue Info—we need to transform these cues into tracks, then save the tracks as discrete WAV files.

5. In the lower-right corner of the Cue List window, click Batch. This brings up the Batch Process Phases window (see Figure 6.37). Here select the radio button next to Save to Files. Remove the check next to Use Cue Label as Filename Prefix, and type in an identifiable, definite prefix in the Filename Prefix input area (we're using Neb1 to indicate *Nebraska*, Side 1). Select your destination folder—we're choosing our old standby, the WAV folder we've created just for the purposes of audio recording—and choose Windows PCM (for pulse code modulation, another term related to audio CD-standard sampling) from the Output Format scroll menu. Click OK.

6.37 Click OK in the Batch Process Phases window. This produces the files you'll eventually be burning to CD.

Now your waveform is being split into tracks that you'll find in whatever destination folder you chose. Our tracks, when they arrive, are called Neb101.wav, Neb102.wav, and so on).

6. With side two, repeat this entire procedure, but this time, when you get to the Batch Process Phases window, change the Filename Prefix to something else—we're going with Neb2, simple enough. This is to avoid overwriting what you've got in your destination folder from side 1. This time around, our files are called Neb201, Neb202, and so on...you get the idea.

That's it, you're all split. Save what you will, and exit Audition.

The Burn

Open your favorite CD-R software, tell it you want to make an audio CD, queue up your tracks, and burn them. That's it. This is pretty much a standard procedure burn, except that you've probably cleared the silence from either side of your tracks. So, if you decide to burn DAO, remember to leave a second or two of silence between the tracks; TAO will do that for you automatically — or accidentally automatically, as it happens (see Chapter 1 for the difference between DAO and TAO). That's it.

Bob likes to get real complex here during the burn. Before he burns anything, he goes to KFC and gets a deluxe bucket, which he proceeds to eat, saving the bones. Then he drives home, approaches his computer chanting something about "Finger Lickin' Good," and he shakes his bucket of chicken bones at his CD-R drive. Josh just hits Burn, frolics outside for 10 minutes, and then returns to see if it worked. Try both ways, see which way you prefer. Some folks, we've heard, go watch TV during the burn process—you can try that, too.

Recording and Restoring Vinyl

As with any technology, there are good things and bad things about CD. Think of *2001: A Space Odyssey*, where the bone hurled upward by that murderous monkey becomes, through cinematic magic and good editing, a comfy spaceship. We tend to think of CDs as that comfy spaceship—the leap forward—when in fact CDs are mostly bones thrown by murderous monkeys. The corporations that control music distribution left a lot of very important stuff by the wayside when digitization swept the nation: who cares about Allen Ginsberg's *First Blues* and The Virgin Fugs' *For Adult Minds Only* when we got Britney Spears, right? And who cares about the narratives of freed slaves and the blues issuing from their children and grandchildren when we got Justin Timberlake? Well, that's what these corporations figure anyway: a reminder that we're among the most sexually repressive, racist, sexist, violent societies in the world doesn't help the bottom line.

NOTE Didja know: The United States of America, Land of the Free, has more prisoners per capita than any other nation in the world (this, of course, includes Iraq, Iran, Saudi Arabia, North Korea, Russia, Israel, China, the United Kingdom, et al.)?

The record companies chose your taste—your culture even—for you. Sure, you get that nice illusion of freedom when perusing the stacks at Tower Records (and that nice illusion of freedom when you go out looking for a job, and that nice illusion of freedom when you select one useless item of jewelry over the other), but the fact of the matter is, they swept our culture and history under the rug, and made new ones up. And we bought it, and continue to buy it, hook, line, and sinker.

Knowing that, Bob and Josh set out to write this book you're holding, hoping we'd encourage you to restore and preserve our heritage. This chapter is built to show you not only how to digitize and transfer your records to CD, but also how to regain a good degree of original fidelity. (By "original fidelity" we mean what your record sounded like when you or the previous owner played it for the first time.) Of course, that assumes you want to fix 'em up at all: some people leave the digital recordings of the records "as is" to preserve the accrued extraneous sounds accompanying the older medium (that soothing campfire crackle and the occasional pop), and if that's your preference, feel free to disregard the restoration section of this chapter.

Requisite Stuff

If you read Chapter 6, "Restoring and Recording Cassette Tapes," (we strongly suggest you read Chapter 6, by the way, because we'll be referring to it often in this chapter), you'll remember how obviously simple it is to connect a tape deck to your computer. Connecting a turntable isn't much more difficult— most of your choices will be contingent on the hardware you have at hand, just as they were in Chapter 6. One thing you will need in addition to the items we discussed in Chapter 6 is some kind of preamplifier. It can be a stereo receiver featuring a phono-in and a line out (sometimes called "tape out"), an actual preamp, or a mixing board with phono-in jacks and line out jacks (see Chapter 2, "Hardware and Software," for our discussion of these various devices). You'll need a preamp because the signal—that is, the music on your record—issuing from a turntable is too weak, electromagnetically speaking, and must be amplified and adjusted for audible playback. (For more information, see the sidebar called "Phono Preamplifiers.")

Phono Preamplifiers

Say you jumped the gun a little and plugged your turntable directly into your line-in jack. You'd notice that no sound comes out of your speakers, and when you go to record, no levels are present. As you know, or could guess just by watching a turntable, an LP's grooves vibrate a stylus, and these vibrations become sound, immediately, right there. You can hear a record playing even if the volume on your speakers is all the way down, though only just barely, and only if you're standing right next to your turntable.

The vibrations of the stylus become electric signals in the head of the tone arm, and the electrical signals are passed along the tone arm, all the way on down to the tips of the RCA cables dangling from the rear of your turntable. The thing is, the vibrations in the stylus caused by the LP aren't powerful enough to be loud, and the ensuing electrical signals produced in the tone arm head are similarly weak. They must be amplified to become audible. That's the first thing a phono preamplifier does: It makes audible the relatively weak electrical audio signal coming out of your turntable.

Now, let's say for a minute you are able to hear the record playing over your computer's speakers, even though you're not using a phono preamp. You'll be astonished at the incredible lack of bass you're hearing, and you'll wince at the overwhelming treble. That's not what records sound like, right? Well, actually, it is, up until they hit a phono preamp.

Wide grooves on a record slowly and lethargically vibrate the stylus, producing bass notes; narrow grooves agitate the stylus quickly, producing treble notes. The treble grooves are superimposed on the bass grooves to produce the whole vibration in the stylus that constitutes a typical song, bass, and treble. To produce a true bass note, though, these bass grooves must be extremely wide, so wide that if a record were cut to produce true bass notes, you'd be able to get only about five minutes of song on a standard 33 RPM vinyl record.

continues

continued

About 50 years ago, some people devised a way to get bass out of narrower grooves without ultimately losing any fidelity. They figured if they could attenuate the bass in the original signal some, the groove cut onto a record would end up being relatively narrow. So, when a record is being cut—they are actually cut, with a machine called a lathe—a bass-reducing equalization curve is applied to the audio signal coming in to produce the cuts. You've probably performed the application of an equalization curve to an audio signal yourself, using your stereo's graphic equalizer. Maybe you have 5 little sliders on your graphic equalizer; maybe you have 30. Imagine a curved line running through those little sliders, in whatever positions you've moved them to—connect-the-dots, if you will. That curved line is known as an equalization curve. The equalization curve applied to the audio signal reduces the strength of bass signals, thus reducing the width of the grooves that are cut into the record.

It was the RIAA (Recording Industry Association of America) that came up with this curve—yes, the very same RIAA that's coming down hard on the MP3 crowd today. Its equalization curve has been cutting narrow bass grooves since 1953, when it became the standard way of altering an audio signal that's to be cut to a record. Pretty much every song on every record since 1953 is equalized this way.

The mere fact of physical contact between a stylus and a record produces a lot of high-frequency noise—fingernails on a chalkboard, in essence. If those fingernails were playing music, though, and if those music signals were boosted high enough to drown out the screech, the screeching wouldn't cause us to cringe. So, to the end of drowning out the noise of contact (usually called surface noise), treble is enhanced in the equalization curve, in the same way bass is attenuated.

A phono preamp, in addition to amplifying incoming sound signals, applies the inverse of this equalization curve (called an RIAA Curve) to the audio signal coming in from the turntable. The phono preamp boosts the bass that was cut and cuts the treble (as well as the surface noise, those fingernails on a chalkboard) that was boosted during the cutting of the record. In so doing, it brings the sound back to normal, finally yielding very high fidelity to the original audio signal. That's why you need a phono preamp for restoring as well as for listening to records.

It goes without saying that you'll need a turntable—a.k.a., a record player—and some records to undertake this project (see Figure 7.1). You'll also need at least one pair of RCA cables (see Figure 7.2) to connect your turntable to whatever preamplification device you've decided on, unless RCA cable is already dangling from the rear of your turntable (some turntables come with RCA cables built-in). In that particular case, you won't need any RCA cable there—you'll simply plug that pair into your preamp.

7.1 Just in case you haven't seen one before, this is what a turntable looks like.

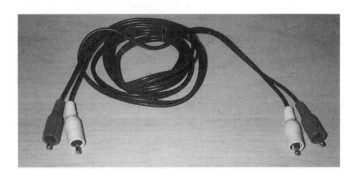

7.2 Nothing fancy yet, just plain old RCA cable.

If you intend to clean up your recording, you'll also need a digital audio editor (DAE), either the one that came with your CD-R software bundle or a stand-alone product. (See Chapter 2 for a list of DAEs and CD-R software we recommend.) For this project, we'll be using DC Five (www.tracertek.com), a stand-alone digital audio editor (see Figure 7.3). We've found it's the single best product on the market for restoring analog material. (In fact, the manual alone is worth the price of the package.) As we mentioned in pretty much every other chapter, digital audio editors all look the same, so it should be pretty easy for you to follow along, regardless of what you're working with.

7.3 DC Five is the most recent iteration of the best vinyl restoration package available. It used to go by Diamond Cut. (That's what "DC" stands for, we assume.)

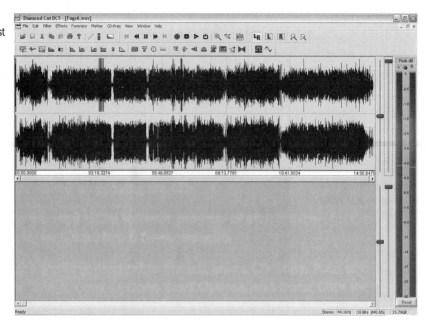

Don't do this yet (or do, if you want, but make sure everything's unplugged), but after you've plugged your turntable into your preamp device, you'll need to run some kind of cable between your preamp and your sound card or USB audio capture device (also discussed in Chapters 2 and 6). One thing about this cable—it'll be either RCA or Y-Cable, exactly as in Chapter 6—is that it needs to be long. Three to five feet should do it. The reason for this is you're going to want to keep your turntable-preamp rig as far away from your CPU, monitor, and powered speakers as possible. Your machine regularly fires off electromagnetic noise, which gladly attaches itself to your recording. You don't want that: there's already enough noise to work with here, the last thing you need is more.

Finally, and optionally, you may wish to obtain a record cleaner. These things come in many forms, ranging from mini-vacuum cleaners, solutions, and brushes, to weird things that drop beads of water that are then picked up by a piece of string. Each will be accompanied by instructions, so no worries there. In this chapter, we'll be cleaning our vinyl the old fashioned way: chamois and distilled water. But first...

Hooking Up

Power down and unplug everything on your strip or UPS—CPU, speakers, fax, printer, monitor, everything. By the time we get around to plugging things back in, you should have only five things plugged in to your power strip: the turntable, the preamp device, your CPU, your monitor, and your speakers.

The first thing you'll want to do is set up your turntable-preamp rig. You'll have to eyeball things a bit here: make sure the distance from this rig to your computer is close enough for a cable to reach your sound card, but far enough away to elude stray electromagnetic emission from your computer. Now you need to do three things:

1. You'll need to run the previously mentioned RCA cable from your turntable's phono-out to your preamp device's phono-in.

2. Ground your turntable. Often on a preamp or mixing board, there's a peg or plug on the back that's either marked "Ground" or says nothing at all. You'll find a similar thing on the back of your turntable. Between those two pegs, plugs, whatever they are, run a piece of copper wire (speaker wire will do; simply strip a piece).

   Grounding prevents hum and buzz, which we'll discuss in a moment. If it happens you don't have pegs or plugs, and you're getting hum or buzz after everything's hooked up and plugged in, run a piece of copper wire from the metal chassis of the preamp device to the metal chassis of the turntable. You can just tape it down, if you want, or you can loosen screws on each item, wrap the wire around it, and then tighten the screws.

   Stay unplugged!

3. From your preamp device, then, you'll run that longer piece of cable we discussed earlier from the line-out (or tape-out) of your preamp to your sound card or other audio capture device. You have exactly the same options here as you did in Chapter 6:

   ○ **Mini-jack to line-in:** Again, for this, you'll need either a Y-cable or RCA cable with a stereo-mini adapter at one end (see Chapter 6 for further details on those cables). Plug the RCA cable end into your preamp's line-out, and plug the stereo-mini end into your sound card's line-in.

○ **RCA:** If your sound card features an RCA line-in, simply run a piece of RCA cable from your preamp to your sound card. We'll again refer you to Chapter 6 for more details on those cables and that connection.

○ **RCA to USB:** Audio capture device: exactly the same as RCA.

Now you can plug your stuff in. As we mentioned in Chapter 6, plug everything in to the same power strip to avoid hum and buzz. Hum and buzz are discussed in detail in Chapter 6, and we'll discuss it again later in this chapter, in the "Restoring" section.

Scrub Before Surgery

Now we're going to play one side of your record over your computer's speakers without recording anything, or anything you'll keep, anyway. The reasons for this are legion:

○ You'll see, or hear, rather, whether or not you've succeeded in connecting properly.

○ You'll have the opportunity to configure your computer's sound controls (read the "Preparing for Recording" section in Chapter 6 for a thorough and illustrated explanation).

○ You'll hear the faults in your record (skips and such, which we'll show you how to fix).

○ You'll be dislodging dirt from the grooves on your record.

TIP

If you're using a mixing board as your preamp, turn your levels way, way down, a little bit above all the way down, and then bring them up later, very slowly. You won't need much oomph that way. Otherwise you'll likely blow your speakers and shatter glass. Very dangerous for feet, ears and, given the fire hazard, home insurance premiums.

Adjusting Your Audio Controls for Windows

To configure your machine's sound controls, simply complete the following steps:

1. Double-click the loudspeaker icon in your system tray.

2. Slide the Play Control bar all the way up.

3. Slide the Line In bar up to about the middle (and remove the check from the Mute box, if there's one there). Remember you can always come back to this if you're not happy with what's coming through your speakers.

4. Choose Options > Properties.

5. Select the Recording radio button.

6. Put a check in the Select box beneath Line In (or wherever you've plugged in).

7. Close out of the Options menu.

8. Bring the slider beneath Line In all the way down.

   Now you can open up your digital audio editor and begin playing something—here, your record.

9. Record it in your digital audio editor.

10. Gradually slide the Line In bar and check your recording levels in your digital audio editor, seeing to it you don't clip (see Chapter 6, steps 7-10 under "Recording").

11. Exit your digital audio editor and don't save anything. Waste of space.

NOTE If you're planning a lot of recording and restoration projects, a mixing board might be the way to go for a preamp device—you can plug your turntable, tape deck, eight track, and anything else into it all at once. You don't need a fancy one; you can fix most faults using your digital audio editor.

More Cleaning

Once you're happy with what you're hearing over your speakers, and happy with your recording levels, take your record off the turntable for round two of cleaning (round one being that first dirt-dislodging run). The most convenient way to do this is to grab a jug of distilled water, dampen a chamois with it, and carefully wipe your record down. Or, you can use devices designed specifically for cleaning records—the vacuums and such we talked about earlier. You can also find places in your town that will professionally clean your vinyl for you.

Now you should have a pretty clean record. We do, having traveled the simple distilled-water-on-chamois route. Do be gentle if you travel this road, and never, ever use anything besides distilled water or solutions specifically designed for cleaning vinyl.

Working with Warps

If your vinyl is warped, you can do a couple things. The first is not for the faint of heart: preheat your oven to 125 degrees F. Then go to the hardware store and grab two panes of glass, big enough to sandwich an entire record between. Bring those home and place your warped record between those panes and cook the sandwich for five minutes—don't leave it, stay with it—and remember that you're cooking a record. You don't want this dish overdone. Bring it out and let the sandwich cool awhile, a couple hours usually does it.

If that scares you, and it should a little, there's another way. This method will fix problems caused by scratches and warping and is generally safe for use on all records. Grab the loose change from your pocket, and make sure you have one of each coin—penny, nickel, dime, and quarter. Place a dime on top of the tone arm's head (the thing that houses your stylus), and then play the record. If the dime doesn't help the stylus track properly, move on to the penny, and so on, all the way up to the quarter. You want the least weight possible, because this technique will eventually devour your record, and more weight will accelerate the process. Since we're only doing this trick once per skipping record, your tunes should be safe. If it happens that a quarter is called for, but the record, although not skipping, is rumbling something fierce, don't fret: you can get that rumble out with a software filter.

Recording

Put your record back on the turntable, clean side up. Don't play it just yet.

First, make sure your computer speakers aren't playing so loud that they vibrate your turntable. We're totally tempted to pump it here, since we're recording the Virgin Fugs' 1965 release *For Adult Minds Only*, one of the albums we mentioned that failed to meet Corpco, Inc.'s standards of decency (or sales, or something), and consequently failed to make it to CD. Our best guess is that a young Tipper Gore took issue with "I Command the House of the Devil" or "NEW AMPHET AMINE SHRIEK" and saw to it that her buddies climbing the ladder kept it away from us. We don't know, though, so don't quote us on that. The point is, we're resisting the temptation to blare this not because we don't want to offend Jim from Infrastructure Development next door, but rather because we don't want our stylus vibrating any more than it needs to.

NOTE

In all seriousness, *For Adult Minds Only* is one of the finest anti-war albums ever put together, and in our opinion is a thing worth preserving, especially now. However, *For Adult Minds Only* has two drawbacks. One, it attracts cats and anarchists. Naturally, we called the police on the 17 trespassing anarchists, but as we were dealing with that, a cat came in and swiped at the record. Two, there's a drug mentioned on the album Josh has never heard of. That makes the album's credibility suspect.

Let's record.

1. Open your digital audio editor—again, we're using DC Five here—and navigate over to the record function. The DC Five Record function is a red button on the top taskbar (see Figure 7.4). Clicking that button brings up the Record File window (see Figure 7.5), displays your level meters, and offers the typical sample options—sample rate, resolution, and so on.

   You were probably in this window just a second ago when you were checking your input levels; if you weren't, shame on you!

7.4 The Big Red Record button (it's red, not gray, trust us) launches the project.

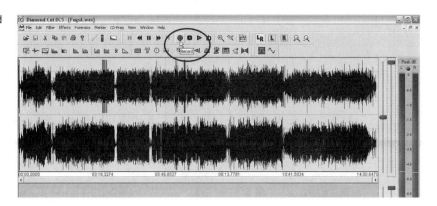

7.5 Here's the Record File window. You may have noticed they all look the same.

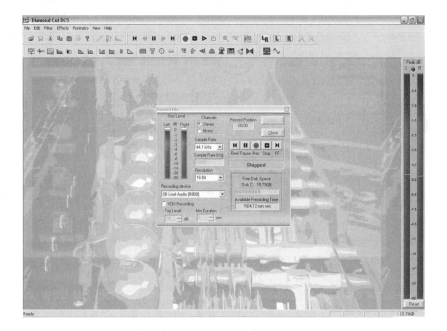

2. In the Record File window, select the sound card you plugged into from your preamp—or whatever other thing attached to your computer that'll be receiving the preamp's signal, such as a USB device—from the Recording Device drop-down menu below the level meters (see Figure 7.6).

3. Select your sample rate (44.1 kHz, you remember) and your resolution (16-bit), and your channels (stereo). That, as you probably know by now, is the CD-Audio standard.

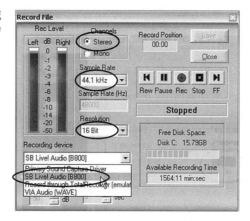

7.6 Here we're selecting our sound card, since the signal from the preamp will be entering there.

4. Click the Record button, and then begin playing your record (see Figure 7.7). Just as with a cassette tape, we'll want a long leading bunch of noise so we can take a noiseprint come restoration time.

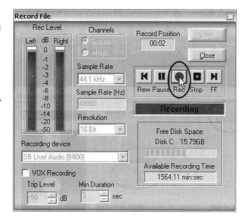

7.7 Clicking the Record button. Do this before you play your record, because you'll want the leading "silence" for a noiseprint (see Chapter 6 for a discussion of noiseprints).

Shortly, you'll have a recording of Side A of your record.

5. Click Save, name it, and close it. We'll save to our WAV directory as usual (see Figure 7.8). This file is huge, so be sure to remember exactly where you saved it.

7.8 Saving side A of our record.

6. Now, repeat this whole procedure—dry run, clean, record, and save—with the flip side of the record.

The entire album should now be on your hard disk, ready to be cleaned and sweetened.

TIP

It may be a good idea to burn these large files to CD, in the event of catastrophe: you'll not only have an "original" copy, but you'll also have something to work with if you botch the restoration.

Restoring

Unlike cassette tapes, records contain all kinds of different types of noise, so things are going to get a little complicated here. The noise reduction filters you'll be using are often open to configuration, and it can be difficult to know just what configurations to stipulate. You've got something we don't, however: you've got your ears, and those, for the moment, are a better guide than anything we could lay before you.

More good news: most audio restoration software allows you to preview results before you apply the filter and to adjust parameters on-the-fly. And yet more good news: anything disturbing to your ear will also most likely be disturbing to a filter, and you'll be notified. Experiment liberally with the filters, and please yourself, above all else. After you've restored two or three albums, you'll find that you've gotten pretty good at it—or at least pretty good at turning out something you're happy with.

We're going to look at the common noises and their respective filters a bit to give you an idea of what they can do and what havoc they can wreak when you're not careful. The filters discussed in the following sections are located under the Filter drop-down menu on DC Five's taskbar.

Clicks and Pops

The filter to remove clicks and pops is usually called an Impulse Noise filter, but you'll also periodically see it called a DeClicker or something like that. This filter is notoriously difficult to configure properly, but you have alternatives.

TIP

Since we'll be taking a noiseprint again, as we did in Chapter 6, you'll need to remove any clicks and pops from the sample where you intend to get your noiseprint. Otherwise, you'll get all kinds of funky results when you run the Continuous Noise and Median filters, which we discuss in just a moment.

Clicks and pops jar everything: your ear if you're listening, and your eye if you're looking at your waveform. They're distinct because they occur loudly, quickly, and unpredictably, but a lot of things can occur loudly, quickly, and unpredictably in music, and that's where problems arise. These filters can also create problems because when they remove a click or pop, they sometimes leave an approximation of what they imagine would be there if the click weren't, which can lead to weird, small, ugly things all over the place.

Because of those potential hazards, a lot of people choose never to use the Impulse Noise filter and instead fix the click by hand. You have many ways to do this, but they all involve locating the disturbance in your waveform—that "picture" of your track—and then zooming in and selecting it for edit. If the noise is short enough, you can cut it out entirely and perhaps never miss that particular segment. You could also simply mute it—your ear, or your brain rather, will close that tiny gap for you by imagining something to put there (a process similar to the one that makes several stills passing by in rapid succession appear to move—as in film or animation). Some software packages will allow you to generate your own sound to paste over the click, and as we mentioned, others will automatically generate what they think would sound OK there.

But if you've got scores of clicks and pops and don't particularly feel like going in after each one of them, declicking might work for you. DC Five features two Impulse Noise filters: the EZ Impulse Noise filter and the Expert Impulse Noise filter (see Figures 7.9 and 7.10). We're not going to use either, but you're certainly welcome to try them out and see what you think. Our guess is you won't really care for the results either.

7.9 This is DC Five's EZ-Impulse Noise Filter. Give it a try if you feel like it.

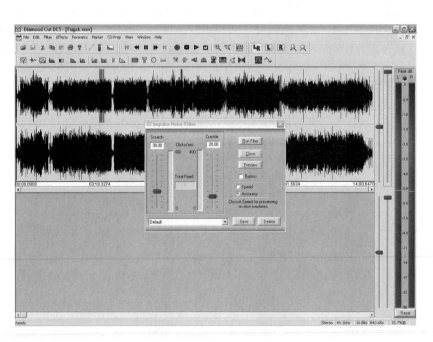

7.10 Here's DC Five's Expert Impulse Noise filter. Again, if you get the itch, try it.

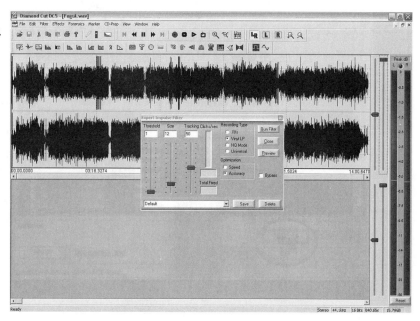

Sampling the Noiseprint

We're instead going to find the sample we'll be taking our noiseprint from, and remove the clicks and pops manually by muting them. Then, if after the application of the Continuous Noise filter to the entire waveform we're still hearing clicks—which doesn't typically happen—we'll go in and mute them manually as well.

1. The first thing to do is find your area of "silence," whether that's the space between songs, or a leading or trailing silence (see Figure 7.11).

7.11 Select a "silent" passage from which to take your noiseprint.

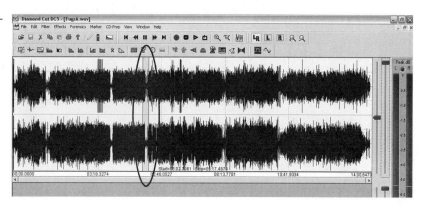

2. Select it by clicking and dragging, then zooming in (the Zoom In button is that little magnifying glass next to the play controls in the top taskbar (see Figure 7.12).

You can see in Figure 7.13 that we've got several distinct pops: they're those big spikes in the waveform.

7.12 Zoom on in.

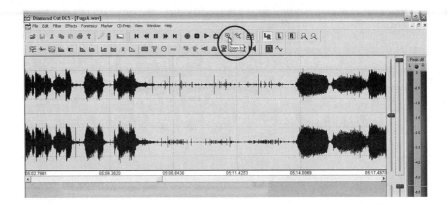

7.13 See those big spikes? Those are clicks and pops.

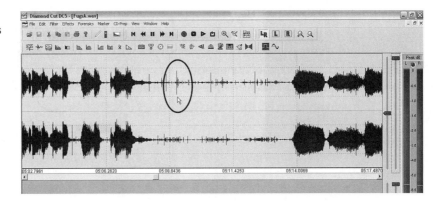

3. Select a small area around the click, and zoom in again (see Figure 7.14). Now your click should be in sharp relief.

4. Select it, right-click, and from the menu that appears, choose Mute (see Figure 7.15).

7.14 Select a small area around the click and zoom in again.

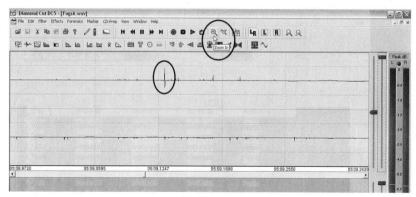

7.15 Muting the click is a simple matter of right-clicking the selection and choosing Mute. Your ears won't miss a thing.

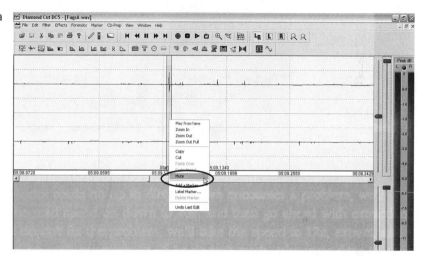

Repeat this procedure with each click. That should do it.

Crackle and Hiss

You'll remember from Chapter 6 that we used a DeHiss filter to get rid of this hiss intrinsic to cassette tapes. In DC Five, the DeHisser is called the Continuous Noise filter. This filter takes care of both crackle—that campfire noise—and hiss.

1. Return to your "silence," sans clicks. Select it by clicking and dragging. If necessary, zoom back on in.

2. Open the Continuous Noise filter from the Filter drop-down menu. In the Continuous Noise window that appears, click the Sample Noise button in the upper-right corner of the window (see Figure 7.16). That'll be your noiseprint.

7.16 The noiseprint we'll be working with here should cure most of what ails us in terms of hiss and crackle.

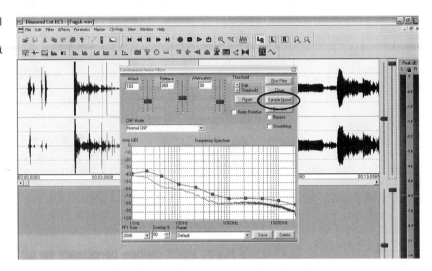

3. Now, click the Preview button. You'll likely still be hearing crackle and hiss. To be rid of it, move the threshold upward by clicking the upward-pointing arrow next to the words "Shift Threshold" in the Threshold area (see Figure 7.17). You'll notice the blue line moves upwards, amplitude-wise.

4. When you're happy with what you're hearing, click Preview again—this stops the filter preview—and click the Save button down below (see Figure 7.18). You'll be asked for a name (we're calling ours FugsA), and then click OK. Your Continuous Noise preset will now appear in the drop-down menu at the bottom of the window.

NOTE

You're probably not going to need to mess around with the slider bars under Attack, Release, and Attenuation here. The defaults are fine.

7.17 Everything beneath the blue (top) line is going to be attenuated. We're moving the blue line up by using the Shift Threshold arrow (see pointer). Keep going up until you hear little to no noise.

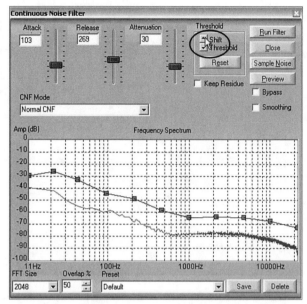

7.18 Save your threshold setting. You'll be applying it to the whole album side.

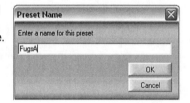

5. Zoom out all the way now by right-clicking anywhere on the waveform and choosing Zoom Out Full (see Figure 7.19).

6. Then, choose Edit > Select All, or simply double-click (left) on your waveform. Open the Continuous Noise filter again, select whatever preset you made, and click Preview (see Figure 7.20). Listen to the whole waveform this way, adjusting your threshold as you see fit. Now and again, check the Bypass box (see Figure 7.21) to make sure you're keeping good fidelity to your original recording. (It'll be all crackly and hissy, but it's good for contrast.)

7. When you're happy with what you're hearing, run the filter by clicking the Run Filter button. That's that.

7.19 Zoom all the way back out. We're going to try our Continuous Noise preset on the whole album side now.

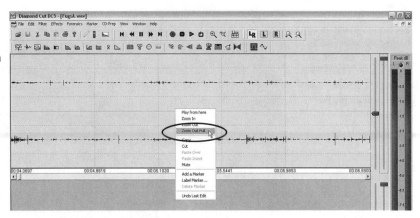

7.20 Open up the Continuous Noise filter again, and summon your preset.

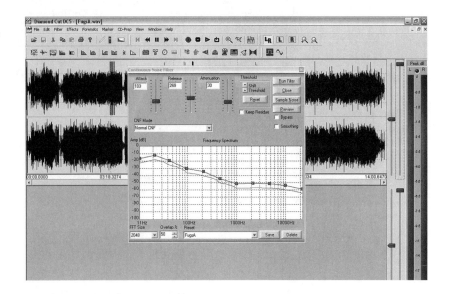

7.21 Putting a check in the Bypass box once in awhile gives you a good idea of what you're doing to your tunes.

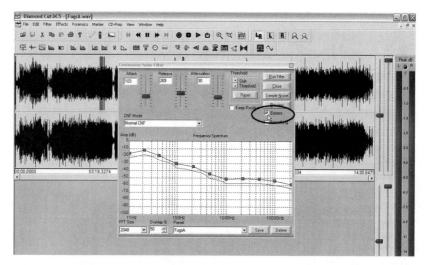

Again, as with all filters, use just enough force to get the sample where you want it; otherwise, you risk choking your track to death. If it's available to you, use the utility in these filters that captures the removed noise. You can then listen to these captives and make sure the filter pulled out only noise and hiss and not any of your music. This is one filter where you'll have to experiment liberally; we can't offer too many tips that won't become obvious during your experimentations anyway.

Rumble

The filter for rumble goes by a couple names: it'll be called either "Rumble" or "Highpass." In DC Five, it's called "Highpass."

A lot of times, turntable mechanics will introduce low frequency noise into a recording—this is generally referred to as rumble, which is what it sounds like. The good thing about removing rumble is it's localized at those low frequencies—sometimes so low that no other information besides rumble could exist there—and can be easily spotted by a filter.

Of course, when you're working at these low frequencies, you're getting close to the bass instruments—keep your eye out for those, and you should be fine. All you should need to mess with here is the slider bar beneath Frequency (as well as your Preview option, so you can hear what you're doing). It's best to keep the Frequency setting really, really low: your best bet is to begin at a 10 Hz setting and move the slider slowly upward until you're satisfied with the results (see Figure 7.22). When you're happy, apply the filter. This will cut—or weaken beyond audibility—everything below the frequency where you finally arrived.

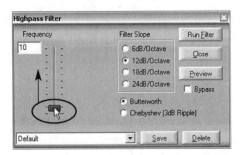

7.22 Fortunately, rumble is easy to be rid of. Start low and travel upwards until it's gone (be careful not to rob your recording of bass, though!).

Again, you don't need to mess around with any of the other controls, the defaults are fine.

Hum

Sometimes you'll notice a distinct hum in the tracks you have copied. Hum can come from just about anywhere: nearby power lines and transformers, household appliances, you name it. If it's electrical and close to your computer, it's a suspect. If you encounter hum in your recording, you'll want to run a Notch filter (also known as DeHum or DeBuzz).

TIP

The most notorious source of hum is a ground loop in your equipment. To avoid these, see to it that all of your equipment is plugged into the same power strip. If you're still getting hum, turn off all but the most essential electrical items in your vicinity and don't be blow-drying your hair while you're restoring records.

One advantage you have over recording studios here is that hum happens mostly in professional-grade equipment, and you may never encounter it. Unfortunately, that very same professional-grade equipment can introduce hum into the original live recording—this hum, of course, isn't your fault at all, but it'll be there no matter what you do, at least during the recording phase.

Since hum is at a specific frequency (60Hz in America; 50Hz in Europe), software can easily locate it and get rid of it. Usually these filters ask that you give a frequency—if the hum is your equipment's fault, tell it 60Hz if you're in the States and 50Hz if you're in Europe, or if the hum is the recording studio's fault, tell it 60Hz if it was mastered in the States...you get the idea. There's a whole host of presets to help you out in the presets drop-down menu at the bottom of the filter. The Notch filter in DC Five (see Figure 7.23) defaults to 60-Cycle Hum—the kind you'll usually encounter—so you don't really need to do anything here except, of course, run the filter.

7.23 Ridding a recording of hum is another straight-forward procedure.

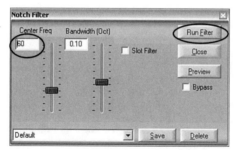

Reverb

If your recording sounds dead in the water, and it's not a result of overapplication of filters (if that's the case, go back and undo your filters, and have another stab), try adding reverb (see Figure 7.24). Most software offers a reverberation filter, which can always helps when a track requires a little life.

7.24 Reverb's always fun to mess around with. Try some of the presets to get an idea of how everything is working. Bob likes St. Peter's Basilica, and Josh likes Small Intimate Nightclub.

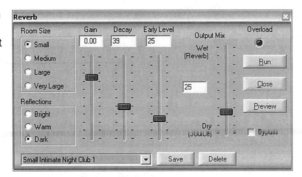

Equalizers

If you got a good track going in, or if you added equalization outside the computer using a graphic equalizer, you'll never need to touch the equalizers most software packages feature. Nonetheless, they can be fun to play with at the tail-end of a project (see Figure 7.25). The results do sometimes surprise you. See Chapter 8, "Polishing Your Compilation Disc," for a thorough look at equalization.

7.25 Another form of entertainment is an equalizer. Got bass?

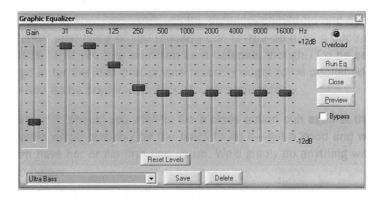

You're Not Finished Yet

Repeat every procedure described in the preceding sections, from cleaning to equalization, with the other side of your album.

Track Splitting

To reiterate our admonition from Chapter 6, we strongly suggest you don't use automatic track splitters, for the simple reason that silence is often part of a song (see Figure 7.26). Instead, drop track markers manually; then cut it up.

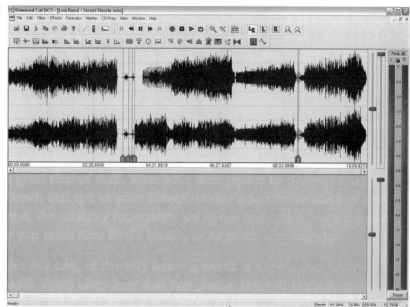

7.26 This is a single song that got split into five separate tracks using an automatic track splitter. You probably don't want that. We don't, anyway.

In DC Five, dropping a track marker is a simple matter of pressing "M" on your keyboard wherever you want to split off a track from the rest of the waveform. You then go to the CD-Prep drop-down menu, and choose Chop File Into Pieces. That brings up the Chop File Into Pieces window, where you're able to select a naming convention (either alphabetic or numeric) for your tracks, a destination folder (we're going with our WAV folder again), and a couple other self-explanatory options (see Figure 7.27). Those options are totally up to you: they won't hurt anything, selected or not, but if you do choose to keep your original file, remember it's taking up a lot of hard disk space. When you're done, click the Chop button in the upper-right corner of the Chop File Into Pieces window (see Figure 7.27).

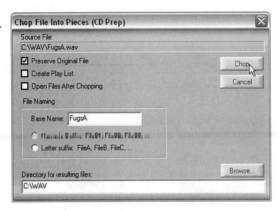

Repeat this procedure with the other side of your album. Your tracks will be ready to burn in short order.

The Burn

Recording your restored audio will be a standard-issue burn: no special steps will be required at this point.

Shut down your audio restoration software and other open programs. Turn off the screen saver and any power management features (those things that shut your monitor down after a period of inactivity). Fire up your burning software. Queue up your tracks in any order you like, tell your software you're making an audio CD, and burn your CD.

Polishing Your Compilation CD

By now, you know how to get a track from your source of choice—tape, LP, MP3, or CD—to your hard disk; you know how to alter your tracks until they suit your ears; and you know how to burn tracks to CD. Knowing those things, you already know how to make a compilation CD, and we don't really need to elaborate further on this subject, right?

Well, sorta. By this point, you should know the basics of making a compilation CD. But most compilation CDs are nowhere near as good as they could or should be—there are pops and clicks from poorly encoded MP3s and snaps and crackles from unrestored vinyl, and most disappointing of all, the sound levels are all over the place. Inevitably, that's how all compilations start, but they don't have to stay that way. There are a panoply of things you can—and sometimes should—do to your tracks before you burn them to CD. This chapter details several tricks and tips—fade-ins, fade-outs, crossfades, and butt splices—as well as a couple of things to hone, nay perfect, your compilation, namely, equalization and normalization. There's even a section devoted to making fake bootleg live CDs.

In this chapter, we're going to use Nero 6.0's built-in digital audio editor, called Nero Wave Editor (see Figure 8.1), to clean up, adjust, and polish our tracks. If you don't have a copy of Nero 6.0, don't panic. You can apply these instructions to the application of your choice. Most things we'll be doing in this chapter don't require the massive feature sets of a stand-alone digital audio editor, and Nero, frankly, is cool.

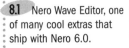 Nero Wave Editor, one of many cool extras that ship with Nero 6.0.

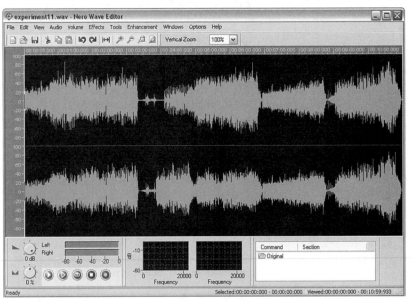

Listen

The first thing you'll want to do is line up your tracks in whatever player you might have handy—Winamp, Windows Media Player, iTunes, your recording software, wherever. Play them consecutively, just as you intend to burn them to disc. A boatload of problems may show up here, for which we have several solutions.

Equalization

You can't get too much treble response from vinyl without getting a lot of noise, too, that being one of the reasons the RIAA Curve was implemented (see Chapter 7, "Restoring and Recording Vinyl"). Even with the treble enhancement during master cutting, though, the treble of vinyl is still a little weaker than the treble of a CD—or other digital media. In fact, CDs evince such incredible treble response, vinyl purists commonly complain that CDs sound "too crisp and tinny." This is because you can get all kinds of treble onto CD without worrying about noise.

When you burn a CD with tracks ripped from digital media and copied from analog media, as we are doing here, you might find that you don't particularly like the contrast between the vinyl, tape, and CD sound. It's just another thing to distract you from relaxation or getting your groove on, or whatever you do when you listen. Once again, this is a pretty easy thing to fix.

Using the graphic equalizer in your digital audio editing software, you have two ways to fix this contrast:

○ You can cut the treble on the tracks you ripped from a CD.

○ You can boost the treble on the tracks you copied from tape or vinyl.

We figure that since the vinyl signal has already been equalized twice—once during recording and again in our preamp during playback for recording—that maybe we should leave it alone now. We usually opt to cut the CD treble as well as the treble of any decoded MP3s we're burning because, as you may remember from Chapter 4, "Recording MP3s to CD," MP3s are most often CD tracks without the unnecessary sonic information.

1. Open your CD track in your digital audio editor. (Again, we're using Nero Wave Editor.)

2. Locate the graphic equalizer, and open it. In Nero Wave Editor, choose Tools > Equalizer.

   You probably recognize the window that pops up: it looks like a graphic EQ you hook up to your stereo (see Figure 8.2). It functions in precisely the same way. Above each slider bar (the frequency bands), you can type in a value to specify what frequencies you wish to work with.

8.2 Nero Wave Editor's equalizer again. It's a lot more flexible than it looks.

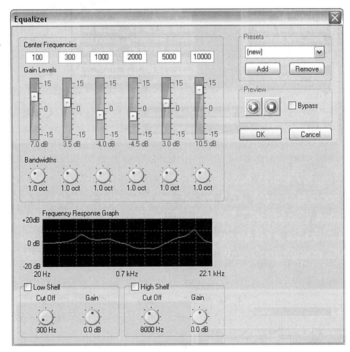

We're going to work with only the two rightmost bands, specifying a couple frequencies: 20,000Hz and 10,000Hz (see Figure 8.3). That's the treble range we're going to reduce. By default, all the sliders are lined up across the middle—this is called a *flat response* and simply means that no equalization will be placed onto your CD track just yet.

8.3 You can alter the frequency bands exactly to your liking. Notice we've changed the values above the two rightmost slider bars to 10000 and 20000. (Those are Hz, by the way, not kHz.)

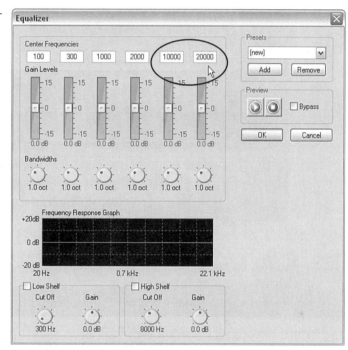

3. You're going to have to do this by ear and memory. Play the track you recorded from vinyl, listening very closely. Doing your best to remember what that sounds like, stop playing it, return to your digital audio editor, and click the Preview button to the right in the graphic equalizer window. Your CD track will start playing (see Figure 8.4).

8.4 Here we've lowered the slider bars to soften the high frequencies of our crisp CD track.

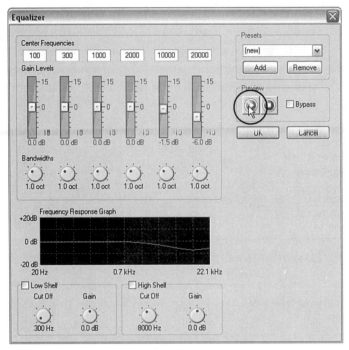

4. Now, move either of those two sliders downward—you'll hear the effect of what you're doing on your track as you do it—until you think you're close to the vinyl sound. Click the Cancel button in the progress meter.

5. Return to your vinyl track, listen to it again, and then go back to your digital audio editor and alter some more, in the way we just described.

6. Keep doing this until you believe your vinyl and CD track will happily coexist on the CD you're about to burn.

7. Repeat this process with decoded MP3s and your tape tracks. Save them to your favorite directory.

Normalization

Next to our CD track, everything else sounds timid: the vinyl, tape, and MP3 tracks are too quiet by contrast. So, if we burn our tracks now, one loud track will appear among several soft ones. This is not conducive to listening pleasure at all. We'll be loudly shocked out of our chairs, just as we were beginning to relax with our freshly burned CD.

This discrepancy in volume happens all the time when you're making CDs out of tracks you pulled from all different sources. Maybe your recording levels were low during the transfer of analog material to your hard disk, maybe the levels were low during the original recording, or maybe the CD was mastered at high levels—it could be just about anything. The good news is, this problem is easy to fix.

All digital audio editing software (and most CD-R software packages) features a *normalize* function. When you normalize a CD, you bring your digital tracks to a kind of "standard" loudness, so that no loud tracks jump out at you from amidst soft ones.

Zsa-Zsa, Eva, and Magda

As we mentioned in Chapter 6, "Restoring and Recording Cassette Tapes," there are three closely related but discrete terms on the subject of loudness: you've got your gain, your amplitude, and your volume.

Gain is also sometimes referred to as *amplification*, which isn't quite right, and is not to be confused with *amplitude*. Gain is defined as the energy of a signal, that is, how much "oomph" goes to your output device, in this case, your software recording of the input. Too much "oomph" causes what's known as "gain overload," "signal clipping," or just plain old "clipping." There's only one cool instance of clipping we know of: there's a nice overload in The Clash's classic "Should I Stay or Should I Go," which caused a great many people to think they'd blown their speakers.

Amplitude refers to all kinds of stuff, usually to vibrating items (your speakers, for example, or your waveform, the electronic representation of what will come out of your speakers). In a ragged nutshell, amplitude (as we've been using it in this book) is the distance an audio signal deviates from silence. Your peak amplitude— the one your normalization filter goes out looking for—is the audio signal that travels furthest from silence. It's from that information the normalization filter boosts (that is, increases the gain of) the peak amplitude to some point before gain overload, and then boosts all other audio signals relative to the new value of your waveform's peak amplitude.

continues

continued

Volume refers to our perception of the magnitude of vibration. It's what you think it is, literally. When you say, "Can you turn the volume down please?" you're translating the phrase, "My sensorial—specifically, my psychoacoustic apparatus—finds the magnitude of the present vibrations too immense for comfort," into English.

NOTE It's a good idea to normalize at the end of the CD-creation process, because tampering with frequency response, as we did just a second ago when we were applying equalization, also alters gain. If you normalize a track first and then apply equalization, you might alter the gain so pronouncedly that you have to normalize again.

Let's get started.

1. Open one of your tracks in your digital audio editor and then locate your normalization function. In Nero Wave Editor, it's located under the Volume menu, and is called Normalize (see Figure 8.5).

   Choosing this command brings up a window with a solitary slider bar.

NOTE In other digital audio editing applications, normalization is sometimes called Gain Normalization, but they both do the same thing.

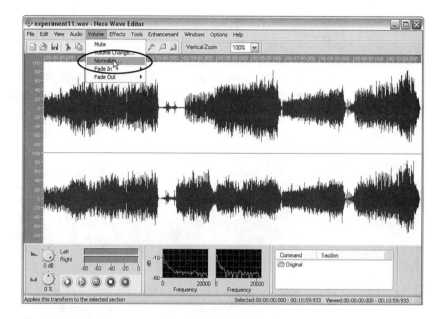

2. Go ahead and move that slider bar wherever you want it, but do keep it on the high side, and do save it as a preset.

3. In the Presets area, click Add, and then type in a name for your Preset—we're calling ours Compilation1). We're moving our slider bar all the way up here (see Figure 8.6)—this, in essence, is the point just before clipping, the strongest amplitude possible. Now click OK.

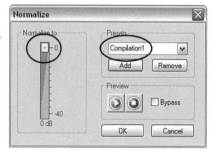

When you apply normalization to a track, your digital audio editor looks for the strongest signal in that song. Once it locates the signal, it brings the strongest signal up to where we instructed it to (0 dB, in this instance), and the remainder of the song will have its amplitude increased relative to that strongest signal (see Figure 8.7).

8.7 The Donovan track is now normalized—it even says so up there in the upper-left corner of the waveform view.

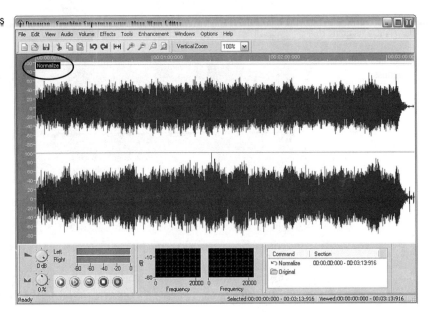

4. Repeat this with all your tracks, using the same preset on each song. Now nothing should lurch out at you sonically.

5. If you find that a few of your tracks are still too relatively quiet, you can adjust their amplitude manually. Again, this is going to be an exercise in listening and memory, though perhaps not as difficult as remembering what's happening sonically at 20,000Hz.

NOTE

The failure of a normalization filter to bring a track up to a suitable amplitude is a common occurrence when you're dealing with the impulse noise (the "pops") of vinyl, where the unfiltered pops often end up being the thing with the highest amplitude.

6. Open your loudest track in whatever you like—Winamp, Windows Media Player, doesn't matter—and then open the relatively quiet track in your digital audio editor.

7. Now listen to your loud track, and try to remember its "loudness" (see Figure 8.8).

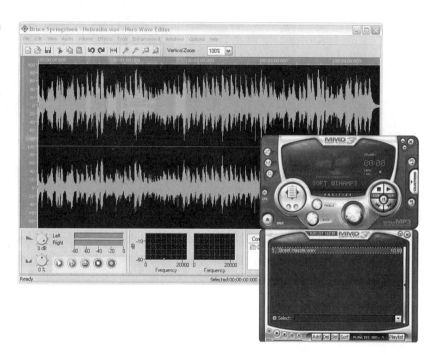

8.8 We're listening to a relatively loud track to gauge and memorize its "loudness."

8. With that loudness in mind, select your entire track in Nero Wave Editor by choosing Edit > Select All (see Figure 8.9).

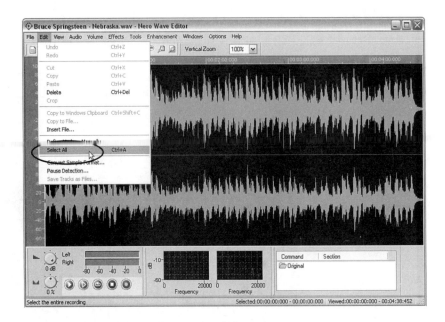

8.9 Select the entire waveform, so you can manually adjust its amplitude with a filter.

9. Now choose Volume > Volume Change, which brings up a simple window called Volume Change. Click the Preview button off to the right, and move the slider bar to the left upwards (see Figure 8.10). When you're happy with your amplitude, click OK.

The Volume Change filter will now process your track, bringing it on up to the volume you found pleasing.

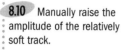 **8.10** Manually raise the amplitude of the relatively soft track.

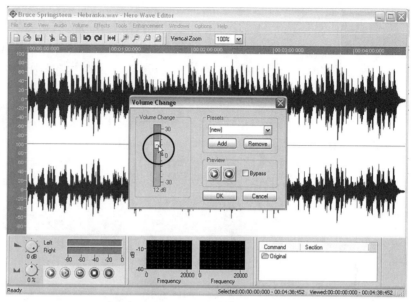

Ta da. That's all there is to that. Let's move on to something else now.

Fade-Ins and Fade-Outs

Sometimes a *fade-in* or *fade-out* is called for. On a track, a fade-in gradually increases amplitude from a quiet, soft starting point, or silence even. Conversely, a fade-out decreases amplitude from a loud point to softness or silence. Traditionally, folks put a fade-in at the beginning of a song and a fade-out at the end, but you can do whatever you want.

Professional recording studios are typically pretty good at discerning when to implement fade-ins and fade-outs, but you may disagree with an engineer's choice and wish to add them where he or she did not. You can also remove them if you don't like them, but that usually results in a strange (or too-dramatic) intro and outro, so we don't recommend it.

NOTE One reason you may want to fade in or fade out a track is to save space if you find yourself pushing the time limits of your compilation CD (usually 74 or 80 minutes). But you aren't likely to know this until you've assembled all your tracks.

To apply a fade-in (again using Nero Wave Editor), we've selected a couple of seconds at the beginning of our track by clicking and dragging. In the Volume drop-down menu, you'll find Fade-In with a couple of very odd options in the submenu: Logarithmic, Linear, Exponential, and Sinusoidal (see Figure 8.11). This is another one of those areas where we'll leave the job to your ears: experiment liberally with each kind of fade, and go with what you like. Josh generally likes vanilla Linear; Bob likes Sinusoidal, just because he likes to run around saying, "Sinusoidal."

8.11 In your digital audio editor, apply a fade-in at the beginning of your track.

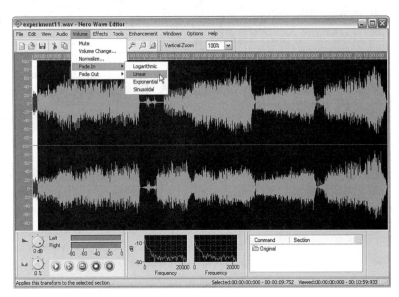

The (Common) Four Horsemen of the Fade

Your ear, of course, is your best bet when applying a fade-in or fade-out, but we'll go ahead and fill you in on what Logarithmic, Linear, Exponential, and Sinusoidal fades are, because those options will pop up again shortly, during our discussion of crossfades.

A *linear* fade-in creates a straight wedge, which results in a steady increase in amplitude from nothing to the amplitude where the fade stops. (Your digital audio editor allows you to tell the fade where to stop.) A linear fade-out, as you may have guessed, is exactly the opposite: it steadily decreases amplitude from the amplitude you've selected to silence. It's the least complicated and most common kind of fade.

An *exponential* fade-in rides low for a long time, gradually increasing, yup, you guessed it, exponentially, squares of squares of squares. It makes for a more sudden increase in amplitude toward the end of the fade-in. If you wish to add a long, long fade-out, exponential is the way to go.

A *sinusoidal* fade-in occurs along a curve, increasing amplitude slowly at first, then rapidly—but not as rapidly as an exponential fade-in—at the end. A sinusoidal fade-out is, again, the opposite. Try this one if you decide to crossfade some tracks.

A *logarithmic* fade-in hits a middlin' amplitude pretty quickly from silence, and then increases only slightly and regularly until its end. Once again, a logarithmic fade-out does the opposite—the song lingers for quite awhile on the way down.

Applying a fade-out is exactly the opposite of fading in, but follows the same general procedure. Just select the end of your track, in the same way we selected the beginning (see Figure 8.12). Now, choose Volume > Fade Out, where you'll be presented with precisely the same options you had in the Fade-In submenu. Again, we're turning this over to your ears now.

8.12 Still in the digital audio editor, apply a fade-out to the end of the track. Fading out works the same way as Fade-in—but here, we're applying it to the end, not the beginning, of the track.

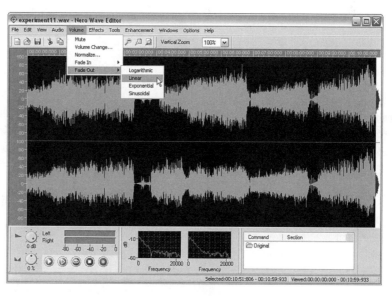

Crossfades

A *crossfade* is that musical moment where one track fades in over the previous track's fade-out, one song slowly (or quickly, depending on your tastes) vanishing into another. You'll need a multitrack editor to perform this operation on your tracks—most digital audio editors feature a multitrack editor and/or a crossfade function, and some CD-R software (Roxio's Easy CD & DVD Creator 6, for one) will automate a crossfade for you during the burn process. Nero 6.0 happens to feature a multitrack editor in its package, called Nero SoundTrax (see Figure 8.13), which we'll be using here.

8.13 This is Nero SoundTrax, a multitrack editor that ships as part of Nero 6.0's array of audio tools. There's no waveform here just yet, simply because we haven't loaded one.

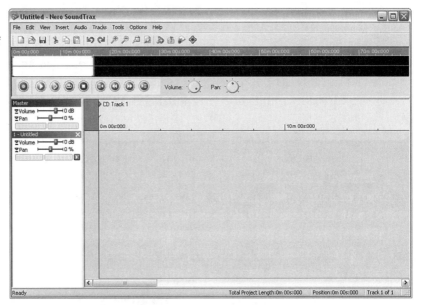

NOTE

Off the top of our heads, we can think of two perfect examples of crossfading: "Sgt. Pepper's Lonely Hearts Club Band" into "With a Little Help From My Friends" on The Beatles' *Sgt. Pepper's Lonely Hearts Club Band* album, and "Carnival Is Over" into "Ariadne" on Dead Can Dance's *Into the Labyrinth*. Spend some time aurally studying those if you get a minute; that should train your ear to hear what's going to fade well into what. You may also just crossfade whenever you feel like it.

For this exercise, we're going to crossfade Bruce Springsteen's "Nebraska" into Lou Reed's "Street Hassle."

1. First, open Nero SoundTrax. (It's located in the Nero 6.0 folder directly above Nero Wave Editor.)

2. Then open a track—we're opening "Nebraska"—by choosing Insert > Audio File, then selecting the track that will be fading out into your next track (see Figure 8.14).

8.14 Select the track into which you want to insert a crossfade. Here, we're inserting "Nebraska" into Nero SoundTrax.

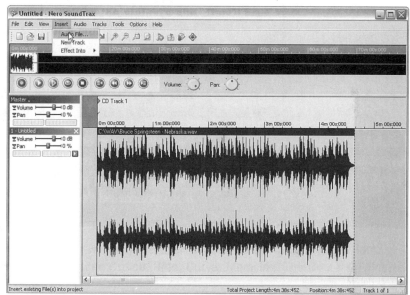

The familiar waveform appears, and you'll notice that you can move the waveform back and forth all you like by clicking and dragging with your mouse. If it's not already there, move your waveform all the way to the left to make room for our incoming track (see Figure 8.15).

8.15 Here, we're clicking and dragging the wave-form for "Nebraska" to the left.

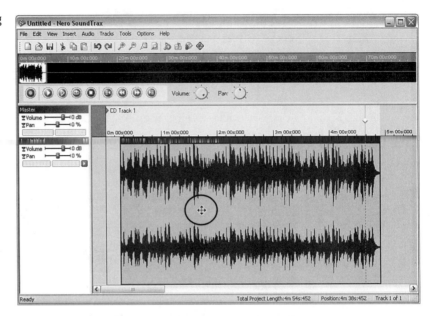

3. Right-click somewhere off to the right of the waveform, in the gray area. From the pop-up menu that appears, choose Insert > Audio File(s), just as you did a second ago (see Figure 8.16).

Your second waveform should appear off to the right of your first.

8.16 Here we're adding "Street Hassle," the track into which we want to crossfade. (It's the wave-form off to the far right.)

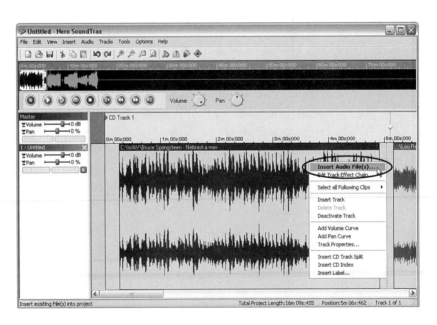

4. Move your pointer over the second waveform, and click and drag it over into the first waveform so that they overlap.

A big red "X" should appear as you do this: this is the area of your crossfade (see Figure 8.17). The right-leaning line of the X is your fade-in, and the left leaning line of the X is your fade-out.

8.17 When you drag one track over another, the crossfade section is represented by a red "X."

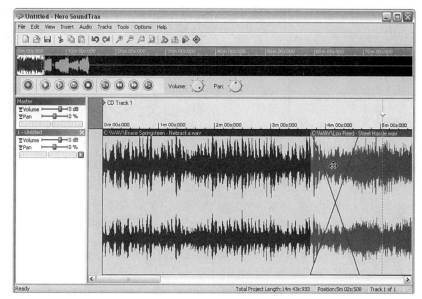

5. Right-click somewhere in the X. In the pop-up menu that appears, you'll see several crossfade options, the very same ones you got for your fade-in and fade-out options: Linear, Exponential, Logarithmic, and Sinusoidal (see Figure 8.18). Choose whichever you like.

8.18 Choose the type of crossfade you want.

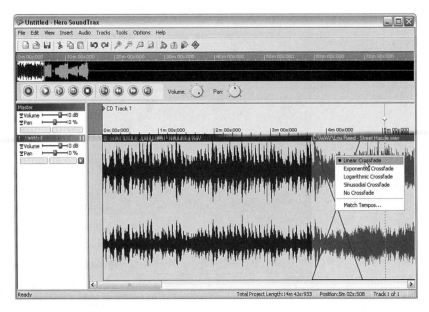

6. Now you're going to have to play around some—dragging, listening, correcting, until you're happy with your crossfade.

If you can't get it to sound good, just forget it—some tunes aren't meant to be crossfaded. This is largely a subjective issue; try it, trust your ears, and be thankful for the Undo function in your audio editor when it doesn't work.

TIP

By the way, if you wish to crossfade all the tracks you intend to burn, you can line them all up in the manner we just described and do your crossfades all at once.

Now you're probably going to want to cut your large waveform into a couple pieces somewhere within the crossfade, unless you want the whole thing burned to disc as one giant WAV file without indices. You can split this thing in two easily enough in Nero SoundTrax.

7. The first thing you'll want to do is choose Options > Preferences to bring up the Preferences window. In the first tab—the General tab—make sure the box next to Automatically Add CD Track Splits is unchecked (see Figure 8.19). You're going to want to do that manually here. Click OK.

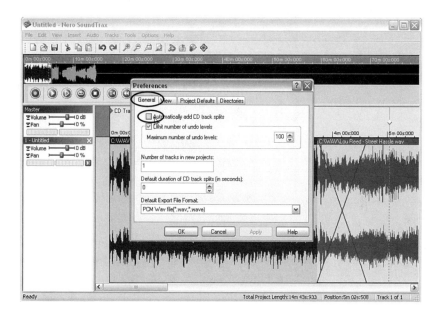

8.19 Make sure the Automatically Add CD Track Splits box is unchecked. We're going to split this manually.

8. Return to your crossfade X and click in the gray area above your track—a little yellow diamond should appear under your pointer, and a line should appear beneath that diamond, perpendicular to your waveform (see Figure 8.20). Try to get that line as close as possible to the intersection of the X by repeatedly clicking in the gray area.

You don't need to be terribly precise here because, either way, both sides of the line will feature your crossfade.

CHAPTER 8

8.20 Put the line and diamond where you want them. (This will end up being a CD track split.)

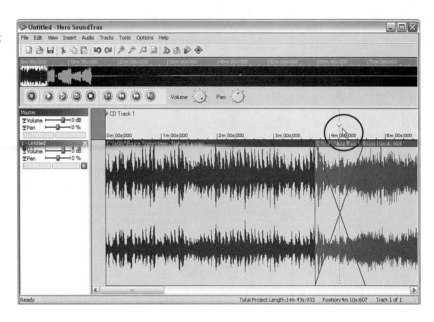

9. Once you're happy with the lay of your line, right-click the little yellow diamond. From the pop-up menu that appears, choose Insert CD Track Split (see Figure 8.21). Now you have two tracks.

8.21 Once you've chosen where you want to split the two tracks, right-click and choose Insert CD Track from the pop-up menu.

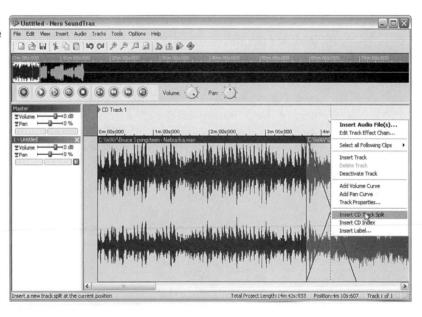

10. Choose File > Export CD Tracks to Audio Files.

11. In the window that appears, specify your directory up top, and then name your tracks in the fields below. We're going to call ours NebraskaC.wav and StreetHassleC.wav (see Figure 8.22). Click OK.

Those should now appear in our destination folder, and are all set to be burned.

8.22 Name your tracks. Be sure to put these two tracks one after the other in your CD layout when burning time comes around.

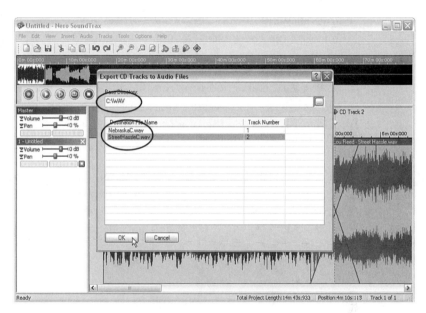

Voila. You've just completed your first crossfade.

ACK!

It's imperative that you burn a disc with crossfaded tracks Disc-at-Once, and make sure there's no silence between the tracks. If you burn Track-at-Once, you'll end up with two seconds of silence between the crossfaded tracks, and that kind of defeats the purpose of including a crossfade. Remember, too, to make sure there's no silence between the two tracks when you're arranging your Disc-at-Once layout. Again, any silence there and you're going to have a funky, mostly silent crossfade.

The Butt Splice

You'd probably be able to figure this out on your own, but, because "butt splice" is to Josh what "Sinusoidal" is to Bob, we'll go ahead and tell you what a butt splice is, and how to make one.

A *butt splice* is two audio tracks directly next to each other in real time—there's no pause between the two tracks. A good example of a butt splice is the transition from "Polythene Pam" directly into "She Came in Through the Bathroom Window" on The Beatles' *Abbey Road*, or "Tame" to "Wave of Mutilation" on The Pixies' *Doolittle*.

All you need to do to create a butt splice is burn Disc-at-Once, seeing to it that no pause is inserted between the two tracks, precisely as you do with tracks you wish to crossfade. During playback, then, your one tune will precipitously become the other tune, full blast.

NOTE

We don't know that this could ever sound anything but cacophonous (which is cool, sometimes), but you can have the end of one track and the beginning of the next track play simultaneously at full volume. All you would have to do is overlap your tracks, as you just did, and tell your software you don't want a crossfade at the merging of the tracks.

Another advantage of the butt splice—besides creating cacophony—is that many tracks have silence built in at the beginning and end. You can enhance the listening experience of your CD by implementing a butt splice (that is, burning Disc-At-Once and setting space between tracks to zero seconds) simply to avoid adding yet more silence between your tracks.

Creating a Fake Live CD

It has been brought to our attention (by Steve, our dear technical editor) that it's quite possible to make a pseudo-live album. In his words, "One cool thing you can do with the multitrack editor is make a fake live compilation, with crowd noise between the tracks, and eruptions of applause after drug or local references, like on those endless '70s live double albums."

This isn't at all complicated. Start by recording or ripping some applause or hooting from somewhere—we took ours from the end of The Clash's live "I Fought the Law"—and saved it as a WAV (by now, you should know how to rip or record a WAV and edit it; otherwise, we've failed utterly).

1. In Nero SoundTrax, open a track with a drug reference. We've got "Mr. Tambourine Man" (The Byrds version) handy, so we'll use that.

2. Choose Insert > New Track (see Figures 8.23 and 8.24).

   An empty track window appears, you can move it about as you please by clicking and dragging.

8.23 Now we're actually doing "multitrack editing"—there's another track waiting to be filled below "Mr. Tambourine Man."

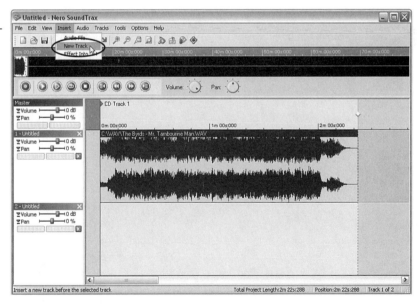

8.24 We're inserting our applause in a random place. Because you can move it around very easily, it doesn't particularly matter where you insert it.

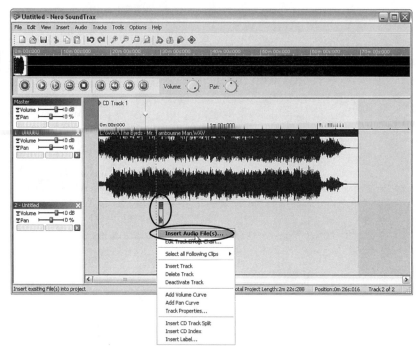

NOTE Your tracks will repeat in a loop if you extend it—this happens when you click and drag the two-pronged left/right pointer on it—and most often you don't want to do that, so be careful (see Figure 8.25).

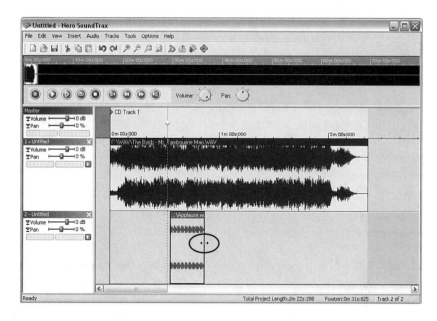

8.25 Oopsies, we just made a really dumb sounding loop out of our applause. Try not to do this.

3. Listen to the track to find your drug reference in the song, stop playing the song, and drag your applause track directly beneath where the drug reference ends.

We've put our applause right after "Take me for a trip..." here (see Figure 8.26).

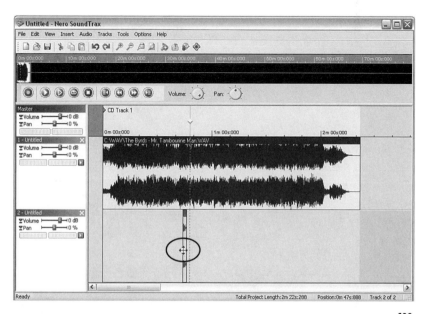

8.26 Moving the applause to its appropriate place.

199

4. Now, return to the beginning of the track and listen to it all the way through. Move your applause as necessary.

TIP

Here, you may also need to tamper with the volume of your applause, either as we showed you earlier in the "Normalization" section, or by using the slider bar off to the left of your tracks (see Figure 8.27). You may need to push the volume upward so you can hear it, or downward so it doesn't overpower the song (or sound artificial).

8.27 Way off to the left of the applause there, beneath the pointer, is the Volume slider bar. If this doesn't work, open your applause WAV file in a digital audio editor, enhance it, save it, and reinsert it into SoundTrax.

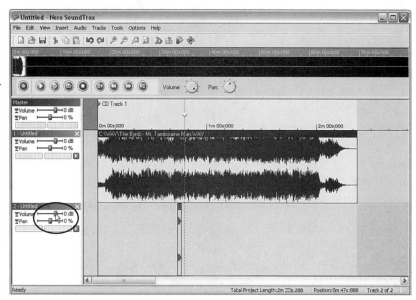

5. When you're satisfied, choose File > Export to Audio File (see Figure 8.28). Save it as a WAV wherever you like.

   You now have a WAV with applause in it.

6. As you exit the program, you'll be asked whether or not you want to save the project. Do or don't, it doesn't really matter, unless you plan to add more applause at more drug references or at the beginning or end of the song.

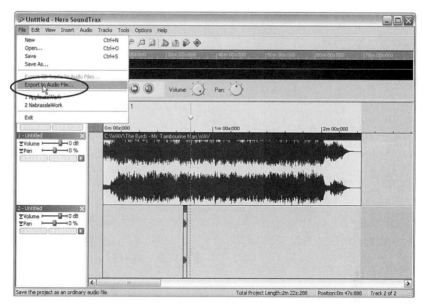

8.28 Saving the project as a WAV with fake applause in it.

The Burn

There, now everything on your compilation CD should sound pretty smooth, sonically. Now you can proceed with burning your CD, which you learned about in Chapter 1, "Diving Right In." Do remember, however, that if you have a crossfade in your compilation, you must burn Disc-at-Once, and see to it that there is no silence between the crossfaded tracks. Once this CD is done cooking, we're going to throw it into the stereo and have a listen. Bob's itchin' to get his groove on.

Creating Enhanced CDs

Perhaps you've noticed, as your computer shakes off its utilitarian fetters and takes its rightful place among your home-entertainment equipment, that bands and their agents are releasing what they call enhanced CDs, discs that not only play in your stereo system but also function in your computer as CD-ROMs. Open them, and you'll see pictures, videos, messages from the band—a whole promotional apparatus right there on your monitor.

We have an enhanced CD sitting right here, a very precious one: Galaxie 500's enhanced version of *On Fire*, which contains all 13 original tracks as well as the video for "When Will You Come Home." We're fairly certain that if we sat in front of MTV for a million hours of broadcasting, or even if we sat through a million hours of more progressive and socially redeeming programming, we'd never see that video. Now, with this miracle of optical storage, we have access to this video any time we like.

CD enhancing isn't just for bands and their record companies anymore. You can make these kinds of discs yourself, using only your burner, your CD-R software, any tracks you wish to record for home entertainment center or car CD player playback, and "data" that can be read in an optical drive. The "data" can be any binary stuff that isn't a track you want to play in a CD player, but rather stuff to be perused on a computer: photographs, Microsoft Word files, ASCII files, viruses, spreadsheets, short films, or anything else that can be represented by 1s and 0s. Essentially, you'll be creating an audio CD and a CD-ROM all on the same disc.

The type of disc we'll be showing you how to create in this chapter goes by many names, much like Josh, who, over the course of a remote dissolute past, earned many names, ranging from the quaint to the obscene. Officially, these are known as "CD-Extra" or "enhanced CDs." (We like the latter, so we'll be using that term.)

The Umbrella

Enhanced CDs belong to a family of discs called "multisession" discs. True, enhanced CDs do get a standard all to themselves (called the Blue Book, which we mentioned all the way back in Chapter 1, "Diving Right In"), but are nonetheless, for all intents and purposes, multisession discs, as described by the Orange Book (the CD-R standard; again, see Chapter 1 for our discussion of that). There are a couple ostensibly innocuous differences between a multisession disc and an enhanced CD—namely, an audio and then a data session *in that order*, and a file called info.cdp, which lands in sector 75 of the disc you write—but those tiny differences can amount to big bucks for a band. If a band's jewel case carries the enhanced CD or CD-Extra logo, that band's label has to shell out royalties. More on that in a moment.

NOTE

By the way, royalty collection isn't something you need be concerned with at all. Nobody's going to come to your house and demand royalties. If they do, tell them to leave, contact a lawyer, and have that lawyer file a RICO suit, as discussed in Chapter 4, "Recording MP3s to CD."

Most, if not all, contemporary CD-R software allows you to write multiple "sessions" to a single piece of CD-R media. Most times, when you're ready to create a multisession CD and have your CD-R software ready to start the burn, all you have to do to write a session is leave a box that says Finalize Disc unchecked, or check a box that says Start Multisession Disc, come burn time (see Figure 9.1). In some cases, you'll need to be sure to close the session even though you won't be finalizing the disc. You can then put that same disc in your CD-R drive at a later date and write more stuff on it, and more stuff, and more stuff, until it's full. Hence the term "multisession writing."

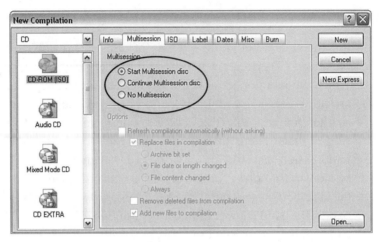

Sessions closely resemble standard closed discs, so much so that you can fool both your computer and audio CD player into thinking it's got only one type of disc in its maw, as long as the disc itself is finalized. As we explained in Chapter 1, an audio CD consists of a lead-in, then the audio data, then a lead-out. That's about all your CD player understands. The laser scopes out the initial lead-in, plays what it plays, then stops at the first lead-out it encounters. That's the way they're designed.

A CD-ROM looks pretty much the same—lead-in, stuff, lead-out—only you don't have an audio area. What you have instead is an area that consists of—for lack of a better term—computer data, whether that be Microsoft's *Age of Empires IX: Age of Imperialist Transnational Capitalist Dogs* or Roxio's Easy CD & DVD Creator 6. (We'll be using the latter for illustrative purposes later in this chapter—see Figure 9.2.)

9.2 Here's the interactive splash screen of Roxio's Easy CD & DVD Creator 6.0. Sneaking a peek at Roxio's market share, we're guessing that this software came bundled with your drive.

As luck would have it, your audio CD player will read only the first session of a multisession disc, stopping at the lead-out of the first session, and your CD-ROM or DVD-ROM will read only the last session of a disc. So, basically, all your enhanced CD consists of is an audio session followed by a data session.

Why does the audio session have to go first? Well, back in the days before there were accepted ways of enhanced CD-making, folks tried all kinds of Rube Goldberg–esque strategies of getting the non-audio content on the disc, with interesting names like i-Trax and Pre-Gap. The one thing everybody agreed on—but only a few were able to do—was that you had to put the "data track" second. CD-audio players froze or cried out in pain when they encountered anything that wasn't music. You could avoid this by skipping ahead to Track 2 every time, of course, but our oral tradition tells us that folks who forgot endured ear-splitting whines and permanent speaker damage.

NOTE
As we mentioned, for a band to carry the enhanced CD or CD-Extra logo on its jewel case, the CD contained therein must have a file called info.cdp written to sector 75. That band or their label also has to pay royalties to Philips, gentle sponsors of several CD standards. Remember, however, unless you're a musician pressing your disc for mass consumption, this isn't something you'll ever have to worry about.

Because they're based on the same principles, you can listen to the music session of your enhanced CD with a software CD Player like Windows Media Player or Winamp.

Gather Ye Rosebuds (But Not All of *Citizen Kane*, 'Cuz That's Too Big)

This used to be much cooler.

As recently as two years ago, creating enhanced CDs was much more flexible, and you didn't have to conform to the Blue Book standard. You could simply burn an audio session, leave the disc open, then burn a data session, *et voila*, there's your nonconformist enhanced CD, *sans* info.cdp. Typically, you'd get a message from your CD-R software announcing that you're stepping outside any known standard, and you'd be admonished not to proceed. You'd then proceed into that uncharted territory, and produce something that can't be found on the books.

For some reason—our guess is that you can't exact royalties on something that doesn't exist, so some powerful someone somewhere gently suggested that he or she might be losing money, and if it's your fault, you're gonna get sued—you can't do that anymore, not with massive market share recording software anyway.

These days, just about the only way to make an enhanced CD is to tell your recording software to make an enhanced CD; there's nothing more to it, except loading up tracks and whatever binary items you've chosen for the data session. Most CD-R software, in fact, thinking on it, all recent CD-R software, to our knowledge, features an enhanced CD (or sometimes CD-Extra, same thing) layout for your tracks and data.

So, natch, you'll need to locate whatever tunes you intend to make an audio CD out of, and whatever you've decided to burn to the data session. Your software will most likely force you to have, at the very least, info.cdp in the data session, and may include various other items. Ignore these or don't, it doesn't make any difference. Put your data wherever you want come layout time. (We'll show you how to do that in just a minute.) Any binary thing you can make a CD-ROM out of can be written to the data session.

A Word on Film

Films, even short ones, are tremendous in terms of the space they occupy. The film we're going to be burning, for example, weighs in at about 10MB per minute, as does Galaxie 500's video. So, keep an eye on that, seeing to it that you leave enough room after your audio tracks for your video track, if that's what you're up to. If, on the other hand, you're simply putting a few stills in the data session, space isn't that big of a concern. It's still a concern, of course, just not as big.

Unfortunately, this isn't a video book, so we don't really have room to discuss such things as shot composition, lighting, the influence of Ingmar Bergman on contemporary avant-garde cinema, capture, projection, frame rate, and so on. We can, however, tell you which photograph and video formats are compatible with both Mac and PC: MPEG-1 and QuickTime for video; JPEG and GIF for photographs. That list is by no means exhaustive, but, because these compression schemes yield relatively small yet good quality audiovisual files, it works well for our purposes.

If you're including video on your enhanced CD, and you've got room, you may wish to include a video player—QuickTime for Windows to play your QuickTime movie on a PC, for example—along with your video. This way, your recipient can install the player on his or her machine, and play your video immediately. "Read Me" files are never a bad idea either, should your intended recipient be not-so-computer savvy.

Gathering your music tracks shouldn't be that big a deal if you've read any of the prior chapters. The audio session you'll be preparing is exactly the same thing as the audio layouts we've been preparing for the last eight chapters.

The only thing you're going to have to watch from here on out is space on your disc. As you know, audio tracks are pretty good-sized unto themselves. Add to that another 10 to 20MB of data, and you've got a pretty full disc layout, if not one so large it can't be burned.

The Layout and the Burn

To show you how create an enhanced CD, we'll use the ubiquitous Roxio Easy CD & DVD Creator 6. It's worth noting that Easy CD & DVD Creator refers to the type of disc we're creating as "enhanced CDs," but other CD-R software applications might have a different name for it. Nero 6.0, for example, refers to this type of disc as "CD-Extra." They're exactly the same thing.

When you open Easy CD & DVD Creator 6...okay, wait, that's too cumbersome a name, so we'll refer to it as "Roxio's software," and we'll use the pronoun "it" as copiously as clarity mandates.

When you launch it, it defaults to a smart-looking window offering several CD-burning options: Disc Copier, Audio Central, DVD Builder, Photosuite, and Creator Classic. Click Creator Classic. The array of options will shrink and attach itself to the top of your screen; then the Creator Classic window will appear, after a brief advertisement (see Figure 9.3).

9.3 This is the Creator Classic Easy CD Creator interface. We understand Nirvana is now considered "classic," too, rendering everything that came before 1989 as "ancient." So, if you're over 15, you're ancient. Sorry to add to the innumerable other adolescent woes.

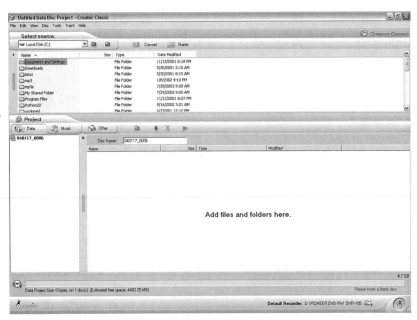

In the middle of the Creator Classic window, you'll see three tabs: Data, Music, and Other. Click the Other tab. From the menu that appears below it, choose Enhanced CD (see Figure 9.4). The lower-left pane of Creator Classic should now read Empty Enhanced CD Project, and you'll notice a couple of folders have appeared where there were none a second ago: one called CDPlus, and the other called Pictures. The Pictures folder is extraneous, that is, it's not in the standard; the CDPlus folder, however, contains the info.cdp file that'll be written to sector 75 of your disc (see Figure 9.5), making your upcoming disc "officially" enhanced. Again, this is important only if you plan on creating thousands of copies of your enhanced CD for resale purposes.

9.4 Choose Enhanced CD from beneath the Other tab.

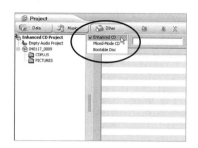

9.5 It'd be nice to have a clean slate for your data, but, as our man Richard Nixon put it, "That would be wrong." That teeny-weeny bit of data, the info.cdp file, is what entitles Corpco, Inc. to royalties. If you're creating your enhanced CD for personal use, don't worry about this mysterious file—it's fine to ignore it.

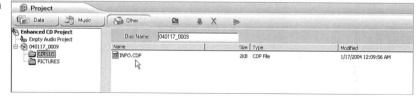

If it's not already selected, go to the top of the Creator Classic window, click the Select Source drop-down menu, and choose the drive that contains your media. Just below the Select Source menu, you'll see a tiny right-pointing arrow. Click the arrow (see Figure 9.6). A display of the contents of your source hard disk will appear. We're doing this simply to make your hard disk easier to navigate.

9.6 Clicking on the right-pointing arrow spares you some hassle when navigating your source disk to locate your tunes and data.

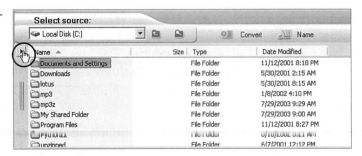

Now return to the lower-left pane of the Creator Classic window. There, click on Empty Audio Project (see Figure 9.7). Drag your audio tracks, wherever they may be, into the pane that reads Add Tracks and Audio Files here. You probably could have guessed that that's where your tracks go, but it's a nice, consumer-friendly gesture to tell us where to put our stuff, right?

9.7 After clicking on Empty Audio Project in the lower-left pane, drag your music on down to the pane where it tells you to do so.

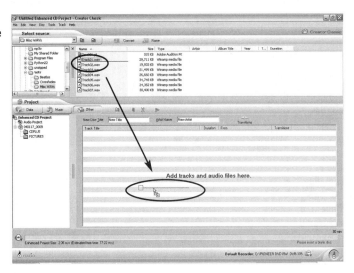

Once you've finished adding your audio tracks, it's time to add your media files, whether you're adding photos, videos, liner notes, or Web site links to your CD. Return to the lower-left pane, and click on the number (it's just a random number representing your disc) directly below what should now be called Audio Project (see Figure 9.8). The pane off to the right, where you dragged your audio tracks, will go nearly blank, save for the two intractable and indelible folders, Pictures and CDPlus (If you happen to poke around in the CD Plus folder, you'll find the info.cdp file we mentioned earlier.) Just as before, locate your data, and drag it into the pane. (We've selected the most important 3 minutes and 22 seconds of film ever shot for our project.)

9.8 Now we're moving on to the data session by selecting the random number appearing beneath Audio Project.

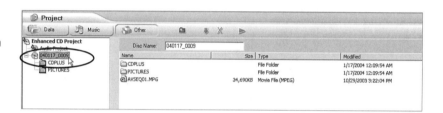

Now all you have to do is burn the CD. You do this in Creator Classic by clicking the small orange button with the Roxio logo on it in the far lower-right corner of the main pane (see Figure 9.9). This brings up the Record Setup window, where you may fool around as you wish (we're pretty sure you know what all this stuff is by now). Click OK when you're all set. You'll shortly have a bona fide enhanced CD.

9.9 Burning at the touch of a button! Sweet! Back in our day, we had to carry 300-pound recorders up 100 flights of stairs in our bare feet, and if we messed up the $100 piece of media, we were beaten with bamboo canes that were soaked for a month in brine and cow offal.

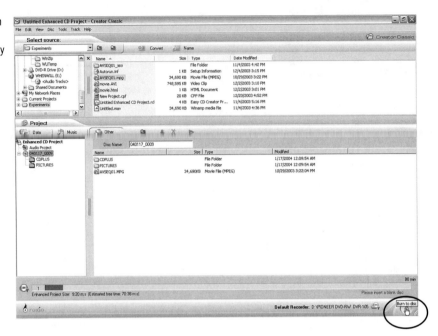

Tips, Tricks, and Troubleshooting

"My computer doesn't recognize my recorder!"

First, make sure the cables are plugged in. Seriously. We all space now and then and the simplest stuff eludes us. The first troubleshooting rule for all computer problems is "Is the thing plugged in?," although Josh would argue that that may depend on what the definition of "is" is.

When installing a new internal recorder, try this first: power down, make sure the little black pin out back is clipped onto Master, attach the drive to your secondary IDE cable, and give it juice. Now boot. If that doesn't work—you'll know it didn't work because it won't be listed with your other drives in My Computer—power down again, and try making it a Slave (move the little black pin to Slave) on the primary IDE cable (the one your hard drive is attached to), and attach any other devices you may have as a master or slave on the secondary IDE cable. That usually does it.

If that doesn't work, fiddle with the cables, IDE, power, and so on until you get a good boot with all drives registered. Shouldn't take more than four tries.

"My drive won't record anything!"

This is one of those questions where most of the time we have to be there to see what's what. Most often, the trouble is:

○ In your hardware—that is, the drive itself. If it's registering on your machine, the problem may lay in your firmware—that is, the recorder's own little bit of programming. To update your firmware, find out the brand of your recorder, either by popping it out and inspecting it, or by looking at its listing in your Devices, and go to the manufacturer's web site. There, you should find an upgrade for your firmware. You simply download it and execute it.

○ In your software. The software you have may not support your drive. This is another easy fix: go to your software manufacturer's web site and find the upgrade that supports your drive. Another problem here may be that you've set your software to Test or Simulate instead of Record.

○ In your OS. If you're running a bunch of programs in the background, or if you don't have a lot of RAM, that could be the thing.

"What gets recorded sounds awful!"

This can result from a lot of things. Our advice (or Josh's advice, anyway) is to listen to your tracks on your hard disk before you burn them. If they're bad on your hard disk, something went wrong during recording, in the case of vinyl or cassette tapes; during extraction, in the case of copying tracks from existing CDs; or during decoding, in the case of MP3s. The solution there is to do everything all over again, exercising a little more caution.

If the tracks sound good on your hard disk but terrible on the CD you burn, the problem is with your CD-R software. The fix here is to burn at a lower speed.

"My recorder says my blank disc is not writable or will not recognize my blank disc!"

Most commonly, this happens because you've got a piece of bad media. Try another piece of media, and another, and another. You may have picked up a bad batch of media. If it's just the one, good; if it's the batch, return it.

Another thing that happens from time to time is your media isn't blank at all (this happens to Josh constantly). Make sure nothing is written to the disc in your drive by either trying to play it or seeing what's on it. You can also eject and inspect: dye that has been written upon is a slightly different color from unwritten dye.

One final thing: keep your fingers away from the writing surface, especially toward the center of the disc. The TOC will be stored there, and without a TOC, or a place to write one, the media is as good as ruined. You can rinse it off, though, hub to edge, with a soft towel and soap. See if that works.

"What's this 'Buffer Un derrun' message?!"

A buffer underrun merely means that the source of your files cannot move them fast enough to the recorder. Thankfully, today most recorders use BURNProof or a similar technology to prevent buffer underruns. Make sure BURNProof is turned on in your recording options.

If you still get the error message, your recorder may be having another problem, and the software is interpreting it as a buffer underrun.

If you have an older recorder without antibuffer underrun technology, you'll have to write at a lower speed.

"My system keeps locking up during recording!"

Some recording programs use proprietary functions that are not necessarily OS friendly, nor do they coexist well with other recording programs. If you are experiencing this problem, we recommend that you uninstall all your recording programs and just install and use a single program. If you must use more than one recording program, reinstall the others one by one. Once the problem occurs again, you have found the culprit, or at least one of them. Uninstall the last program, and you should be ready to burn again.

Keep in mind that software can often leave a trace of itself on your PC, which may cause the problem to persist. If you know when you installed the offending software, one way to undo the evil it has wrought on your recording and well-being is to do a System Restore to a point before the software's installation. (This applies only to Windows users.) You'll find System Restore under Control Panel > Performance and Maintenance. This may help with the detritus left by hardware and driver installs as well.

"My disc skips during playback!"

That's probably an indication of a dirty or damaged disc. Try cleaning it: run it under the sink, gently rub some hand soap on it, rinse it off, and pat it dry. If that doesn't work, you might have to either copy the disc, or extract the tracks at a low extraction speed and make another copy.

Incidentally, the cleaning with soap and water thing often works on store-bought CDs as well. Again, if that doesn't work, extract the disc at a low speed, and then burn a copy. That should fix it.

You may have heard the rumor that toothpaste rubbed on a scratched or skipping CD fixes it. That's not true. All that does, come playing time, is fling little particles of toothpaste all over the innards of your CD player, possibly causing irreparable damage to your machine.

"The CD I burned plays fine in my machine, but not in my stereo!"

Well, there are a couple of things that could be going on. First, you might have made a Track-at-Once disc and not finalized it. Second, you could be using CD-RW media and your CD or DVD or car player just will not recognize it. Unless you have a compelling reason, always use CD-R discs for your audio copies or compilations.

"My drive won't eject the disc!"

Some recording programs may lock your eject function now and then. The best solution is to just close the program and reboot, then eject the disc after the machine restarts. In the worst case, you may have to use the emergency eject feature of the recorder. You might want to make sure you know where the emergency eject hole on the front of your recorder is.

Almost every recorder has a small hole on the faceplate into which you can insert a straightened paper clip or a small allen wrench or any other thin metal object and push gently to manually eject the disc (check your computer's manual). Don't use a toothpick, though. As with toothpaste, a toothpick's cleansing properties don't apply to CD recorders. If the pick breaks off, it may plug up your emergency eject hole, and the only way to fix it will be to at least partially disassemble the recorder. We don't recommend that, even though Bob's curiosity causes him to disassemble any recorder he sees just to observe what is inside.

"There's interminable silence between my tracks!"

Most recording programs allow you to set the length of silence between audio tracks if you're burning DAO. Make sure this is set to whatever you are comfortable with whether it be two, three, four, or five seconds. Keep in mind that many audio tracks have a few seconds at the beginning or end. Sequential tracks with silence at the end and silence at the beginning, plus two or more seconds of recorder-inserted silence can be a bad combination.

"Should I check that little 'CD Text' box I keep seeing?"

Sure! Then be sure to fill in the Title and Artist fields. When you play this disc on a CD-Text capable CD Player, the title of the album and the artist will be displayed. This is handy if you have one of those 100-disc carousels, provided, of course, that the carousel is capable of reading CD Text.

"Can I record and restore my 8-track cassettes and reel-to-reel tapes?"

Sure! Just follow the steps in Chapter 6, "Recording and Restoring Cassette Tapes." Only two contemporary devices require a preamp—a turntable and a microphone—as discussed in Chapter 7, "Restoring and Recording Vinyl." Mikes don't require an inverse RIAA Curve, so all you have to do is amplify that signal. (Which, by the way, is built into your system: your Mic port by default adds 20dB gain to anything coming in. You can turn that 20dB boost off, even, and use your Mic port as a line in.)

Index

X-Y-Z